# The Acquisition of Syntax
# in Children from 5 to 10

# The Acquisition of Syntax in Children from 5 to 10

CAROL CHOMSKY

Research Monograph No. 57
**THE M.I.T. PRESS**
Cambridge, Massachusetts, and London, England

# Foreword

This is the fifty-seventh volume in the M.I.T. Research Monograph Series published by the M.I.T. Press. The objective of this series is to contribute to the professional literature a number of significant pieces of research, larger in scope than journal articles but normally less ambitious than finished books. We believe that such studies deserve a wider circulation than can be accomplished by informal channels, and we hope that this form of publication will make them readily accessible to research organizations, libraries, and independent workers.

Howard W. Johnson

# Preface

This book is a modified and expanded version of my doctoral dissertation, "The Acquisition of Syntax in Children from 5 to 10," completed at Harvard University in 1968, under the supervision of Professor Roman Jakobson.

This work is exploratory in nature. Studies of language acquisition have not yet dealt systematically with the learning of complex syntactic structures. My purpose was to devise means for studying this problem, and to determine their feasibility. The study is limited to small samples, so that the attempt to sketch developmental stages can at best be suggestive. The particular syntactic structures selected for study reflect more the state of knowledge in the field of linguistics than the field of language acquisition, for knowledge of child grammar is as yet too rudimentary to guide such a selection. The work shows that the process of acquisition of syntactic structures does continue actively during the early school years, but in this preliminary form, it does not furnish a general description of children's grammar within this period. Rather it covers specific aspects of the acquisition process in relation to notions of linguistic complexity, treating a number of structures in depth. The results help to clarify the original notions of complexity on which the study is based, as well as yielding insights into the acquisition process itself.

# Acknowledgments

I would like to express my gratitude to Roman Jakobson for the very great assistance he has given me at every stage of this work, for his help in suggesting fruitful lines of research, and for his insightful contributions to the interpretations of the empirical results. I would also like to thank Wayne O'Neil for his pertinent suggestions which helped to clarify many of the notions contained herein.

I am grateful also to Miss Henrietta Brebbia, principal of the Davis School in Newton, Massachusetts, who most cheerfully permitted me to interview the lively and energetic children in her school, and who was always helpful in arranging convenient conditions which enabled me to carry out the experiments on which this book is based. In particular my thanks go to the children themselves, who participated so readily in the language games that we played together on the stage at the back of the library, and who so willingly searched their minds for answers to the sometimes confusing questions that I asked. I wish to thank also Dr. Lester Goodridge, principal of the Bridge School in Lexington, Massachusetts, and Mr. Stevenson, principal of the Parmenter School in Arlington, Massachusetts, who were kind enough to offer me the facilities of their schools for some brief follow-up interviews.

A substantial debt of gratitude goes to my husband, Noam Chomsky, who suggested the topic of this work, who provided major insights as it went along, and who managed, in spite of the overwhelming preoccupations of profession and politics, to pay attention to its progress.

C. C.

# Contents

# 1 Introduction

This study deals with several aspects of the acquisition of syntactic structures in children between the ages of 5 and 10. It is concerned with the general question of the extent to which children in this age group have achieved mastery of their native language, and explores areas of disparity between adult grammar and child grammar. We find that the grammar of a child of 5 differs in a number of significant respects from adult grammar, and that the gradual disappearance of these discrepancies can be traced as children exhibit increased knowledge over the next four or five years of their development. The method of inquiry is designed to ascertain the child's competence with respect to the grammatical structures under investigation, and undertakes an active exploration of his comprehension by means of questioning and discussion. A number of grammatical structures are investigated which are present in adult grammar and are part of ordinary language usage, but which are found to be absent in the grammar of 5-year-olds. These structures are studied in the grammar of children up to the age of 10, when the children's command of the structures is found to approach that of adults. The stages found in the intervening years reveal an interesting and orderly picture of gradual acquisition.

A common assumption among students of child language has been that the child has mastered the syntax of his native language by about age 5. Accordingly most of the research carried out in the area of acquisition of syntax has concentrated on children under 5 years of age, dealing with the period of rapid progress and more readily observable changes in the child's degree of knowledge. Summaries and discussion of the literature dealing with this early period are presented in several comprehensive works, among them Slobin (1967) and McNeill (in press).

Our study deals with the later period, after age 5. Clearly, by this age the rate of acquisition of syntactic structures has decreased markedly, and differences between the child's grammar and adult grammar are no longer so readily discernible in the child's spontaneous speech. Such differences are brought to light, however, when we begin to explore the child's comprehension of particular syntactic structures. Under direct examination, the child's lack of knowledge of a number of constructions which are commonplace to the adult becomes apparent. The process may be viewed as analogous to a study of an individual's vocabulary range. Differences in command of vocabulary between children and adults are revealed more readily by tests based on words of increasing difficulty than by observations of spontaneous conversation. Similarly, differences in command of syntactic structures can be revealed most readily by comprehension tests involving selected constructions of a relatively complex nature. The children's observed failure to correctly interpret a number of such constructions is indicative of several areas in which their underlying syntactic knowledge falls short of the adult's. Furthermore, the nature of the children's mistakes in interpreting these constructions is important in bringing out various aspects of the implicit linguistic knowledge which they do possess. For we find that the children do in fact assign an interpretation to the structures that we present to them. They do not, as they see it, fail to understand our sentences. They understand them, but they understand them wrongly. The information thus revealed about discrepancies between child grammar and adult grammar affords considerable insight into the processes of acquisition, and in addition, into the nature of the structures themselves.

Our procedure is to elicit information from the child about several test constructions by direct interviewing. By age 5, most children have become amenable to questioning. It is possible to work with them in an interview situation, to enlist their cooperation in carrying out tasks, playing games and answering questions, all geared to revealing various aspects of their knowledge of the syntactic structures in question. We find them quite willing, even eager, to participate in such activities, and the interview acquires the spirit of interesting play. We are thus able to observe a variety of responses indicative of the children's interpretations of the structures under study. We select four constructions which are part of ordinary language usage but which we consider, on the basis of notions of linguistic complexity, to be candidates for late acquisition. We test the comprehension of these constructions in a group of children starting with age 5, at which age most children give evidence of not yet knowing the constructions. We continue to test children of increasing ages up to the point at which we find that most children exhibit a command of the structures comparable to that of adults, about age 10. Of particular interest in our observations is that variation in age of acquisition does not seem to affect order of acquisition for particular constructions. A number of related structures, for example, are observed to be acquired by all children tested in the same order, illustrating areas in which linguistic development, whether it occurs earlier or later, nevertheless proceeds along similar paths. Our sample consists of forty children, in kindergarten through grade 4, interviewed at elementary schools in the Boston area. In the report which follows, the theoretical considerations of complexity which underlie the choice of structures are discussed in detail, the experimental method is described fully, and results are presented together with transcriptions of representative interviews with the children.

Recent work in the field of generative transformational grammar has provided the motivation for a study of this sort, as well as the grammatical insights and material necessary for its development. Briefly we may say that the mature speaker who knows his language has internalized an intricate and highly complex set of rules which constitute the grammar of his language. A child who is acquiring language has the task of constructing for himself a similar set of rules which will characterize the language that surrounds him and enable him to use it for both speaking and understanding. When the child speaks, he gives us evidence of various aspects of his internalized grammar, but there are certainly many aspects of grammar that are not at all evident from spontaneous speech. Just as the vocabulary that we comprehend exceeds that which we may ever produce in speaking, the grammatical constructions that we understand are of a greater variety and perhaps a greater complexity than we may ever produce. Work in generative grammar over the last decade has considerably extended our knowledge of the depth and nature of the complexities of grammatical structures, and has given rise to the suspicion that the child of 5 or 6 may still not have mastered certain — perhaps surprisingly many — aspects of the structure of his language that the mature speaker takes for granted and commands quite naturally. Very little syntactic questioning has been done with children of this age, perhaps because until recently the notions of the complexities of language were not sufficiently developed to permit the selection of grammatical constructions which might be candidates for late acquisition. Examples of this nature may now be found in the literature of the field of generative grammar, if one undertakes to examine the literature with an eye to questions of language acquisition. Structures which have potential for late acquisition would be those, for example, which deviate from a widely established pattern in the language, or whose surface structure is relatively inexplicit with respect to grammatical relationships, or even simply those which the linguist finds particularly difficult to incorporate into a thorough description, whatever the reason. All of these might be considered as candidates for late acquisition. Fortunately, a few of these constructions do lend themselves to exploration in young children.

As we have stressed, it is the children's interpretations of the constructions under investigation that we undertake to study. As an example, every speaker of English knows, for sentences (a) and (b),

(a)  John promised Mary to shovel the driveway.
(b)  John told Mary to shovel the driveway.

that in (a) it is John who intends to do the shoveling, and that in (b) it is Mary who is supposed to do it. Many children of 5 or 6, however, have not yet learned to make this distinction, and interpret that it is Mary who is to do the shoveling in (a) as well as in (b). They make this interpretation on good authority, for in fact almost all verbs in English which can replace *told* in sentence (b) require the interpretation as in (b), namely, that Mary is to shovel the driveway: cf. *ordered, persuaded, wanted, advised, allowed, expected,* etc. The fact is that *promise* in this construction appears to be an exception to the general pattern of the language, and most 6-year-olds have just not yet learned this fact about their language, although they do know what a promise is, and are able to use and correctly interpret sentences containing *promise* in other syntactic environments.

By age 8, most children have learned this special grammatical fact about *promise,* and are able to interpret sentences such as (a) correctly. This observation brings us to a clearer understanding of what it means to have learned a word in one's language, i.e., the nature of the information about a word which the speaker of a language has available when he knows the word. There are two aspects to this knowledge, which are distinct from one another. On the one hand, the speaker knows the concept attached to the word, and secondly he knows the constructions into which the word can enter. The child who has acquired the concept of the word but does not yet control some of the constructions into which it can enter gives us clear evidence of the distinctness of these two aspects of his knowledge. A complete knowledge of the word includes both this semantic knowledge and all the syntactic knowledge relating to the word. For a word like *promise,* where there is a particular difficulty attached to the syntactic aspect of the word, we see that the child first acquires semantic knowledge, and later progresses to full syntactic knowledge. It is syntactic knowledge of this sort, which all adults share as part of their knowledge of their language, but which is in a grammatical sense fairly complex or subtle, that we deal with in this investigation.

It is of interest that a study of this kind may be revealing not only with respect to language acquisition, but also with respect to the notions of linguistic complexity on which it is based. We are studying the stage of language learning in which children are at the border of adult competence. The sorts of things that they do know at this late stage bear a close relation to the characteristics and complexities of the ultimate linguistic system that they will one day command. An increased understanding of these complexities is currently developing among linguists and psychologists concerned with general questions of the nature of language and human cognitive capacities. Investigation of the child's knowledge as he approaches linguistic maturity contributes to this understanding and provides additional insights into degrees of linguistic complexity that are otherwise difficult or perhaps even impossible to detect.

# 2 Theoretical Considerations of Linguistic Complexity

The initial task involved in approaching a study of the child's acquisition of syntactic structures after age 5 is to characterize notions of linguistic complexity. The natural assumption is that children acquire later those structures which are more complex. Accordingly, our procedure is first to take up notions of complexity, next to hypothesize on the basis of these notions which structures will tend to be acquired late, and finally to proceed to investigate these structures in children's grammar.

We have found that the results bear out our original hypotheses in many respects, and furthermore that the results contribute to a clarification and a sharpening of our original notions of complexity.

Our approach to the question of syntactic complexity is from the point of view of a listener performing the operation of understanding a sentence. He is essentially acting as a recognition device faced with the task of assigning a structural interpretation to a string of words which he receives as input. It is the specific operation of determining the syntactic structure of the S(entence) which is our concern here. In order to understand a S, the listener must be able to determine the grammatical relations which hold among the words and phrases that make it up. We postulate that the difficulty of this interpretive task is increased by the presence of the following four conditions:

(A) The true grammatical relations which hold among the words in a S are not expressed directly in its surface structure.

6

(B) The syntactic structure associated with a particular word is at variance with a general pattern in the language.
(C) A conflict exists between two of the potential syntactic structures associated with a particular verb.
(D) Restrictions on a grammatical operation apply under certain limited conditions only.

We will discuss each of these conditions, and indicate what structures and test Ss were selected in accordance with them.

(A) The true grammatical relations which hold among the words in a S are not expressed directly in its surface structure.

In order to understand a S, a listener must be able to determine the actual grammatical relations that hold among the words that make it up. When these relations are explicit in the surface structure of the S, as in (1), the task of the listener is facilitated.

(1) John saw Mary.

In (1), the listener has no difficulty in determining that *John* is the subject of the S, and that *Mary* is the object of the verb. These relations are expressed directly in the surface structure of the S by the order of the words, according to the standard subject-verb-object pattern of English, and are readily observable. In some Ss, however, these grammatical relations are not represented in the surface structure and cannot be directly observed by the listener. Nevertheless, he must, in order to understand the S, determine what these relations are. The less clearly these relations are expressed in the surface structure, the more analysis he must perform in order to recover them, and the more knowledge he must bring to bear on the situation.

In the simple case of (1), the subject-verb-object order appears intact in the surface structure of the S. Consider now the familiar examples (2) and (3).[1]

(2) John is eager to see.
(3) John is easy to see.

In (2) standard grammatical order is maintained. To understand this S, the listener interprets that *John* is the subject of the S, *eager* is an adjective predicated of John, and that *John* is also the subject of the infinitival complement verb *see,* i.e., that it is John who will be doing the seeing in this S. In (3), however, this order is not main-

---

1. Discussion of these examples is to be found in Lees (1960) p. 216, and Chomsky (1964) pp. 34–35.

tained. Although *John* appears to be the subject in both cases, closer inspection reveals that in (3) it is the superficial subject only. In (2) it is John who is eager, but in (3) it is not John who is easy. The adjective *easy* is not predicated of John in (3) as *eager* is in (2). In (3) what is easy is for someone to see John. Thus (4) is a paraphrase of (3),

> (4)  To see John is easy.

whereas (5) is not a paraphrase of (2).

> (5)  * To see John is eager.

The deep subject of (3) is actually *to see John*. Further, in (3) *John* is not the subject of the complement verb *see* as it is in (2), but is instead its object. In (2) John is performing the action, but in (3) John is acted upon. In (3) it is someone else who is seeing John.

Thus we see that in (2) the true grammatical relations in the S are far more readily ascertained by an inspection of the surface structure than in (3). To interpret (3) correctly, then, is a more complex task, and ought to require more extensive syntactic knowledge. We hypothesize that the child will learn to assign the correct interpretation to (2) earlier than to (3). We assume that interpretation (2) is the simpler of the two, in the sense of more accessible, or more readily applied, and also earliest learned. For the child who is in the process of learning the rules for interpreting these two types of Ss, we assume that the tendency to assign interpretation (2) will predominate. What this would mean in practice is that given a S of type (3), the child whose rule system is still in a state of flux would tend to assign to it a (2) interpretation. Once the rule system has become firmly established, we would expect this tendency to disappear, and to find that the child assigns the (3) interpretation where required.

The fact that children have more difficulty with constructions in which word order differs from the standard has been noted by other researchers. Luria and Yudovich (1959) describe a case of 5-year-old twins with retarded speech development who interpret passive Ss in Russian as active, understanding *Petia was struck by Vasia* to mean that Petia struck Vasia. The tendency is to interpret the S as if standard order of words is exhibited. This primacy of the active S form over the passive has been noted also in English for very young children by Fraser, Bellugi, and Brown (1963), Turner and Rommetveit (1967), and Slobin (1966).

(B) The syntactic structure associated with a particular word is at variance with a general pattern in the language.

We will now take up a set of constructions in which elements crucial to the understanding of the S are omitted from its surface structure, and must be supplied by the listener. Consider Ss such as

(6) John told Bill to leave.
(7) John persuaded Bill to leave.
(8) John ordered Bill to leave.

In each of these Ss, the subject of the infinitival complement verb *leave* is not expressed, but must be filled in by the listener. In order to understand these Ss, he must be aware that the implicit subject of *leave* is *Bill* in each case. Although two candidate noun phrases (*NPs*) are present in the main clause, *John* and *Bill,* the listener must know to select *Bill* as complement subject. He must have learned a rule for interpreting Ss of this type in which the complement has an infinitival verb lacking a subject. The rule must say, in essence, that

(9) For Ss of the form
$$NP_1 \quad V \quad NP_2 \quad to \quad inf \; vb$$
assign $NP_2$ as subject of the infinitive verb.

Rule (9) applies very generally in English, holding for almost all verbs which take complement constructions similar to (6–8) above. A partial list of examples is:

(10)   a.  John told Bill to leave.
      b.  John persuaded Bill to leave.
      c.  John encouraged Bill to leave.
      d.  John ordered Bill to leave.
      e.  John permitted Bill to leave.
      f.  John allowed Bill to leave.
      g.  John urged Bill to leave.
      h.  John caused Bill to leave.
      i.  John advised Bill to leave.
      j.  John enticed Bill to leave.
      k.  John forced Bill to leave.
      l.  John selected Bill to leave.
      m.  John compelled Bill to leave.
      n.  John required Bill to leave.
      o.  John believed Bill to be a sociable fellow.
      p.  John understood Bill to be a sociable fellow.

q. John knew Bill to be a sociable fellow.
r. John found Bill to be a sociable fellow.
s. John considered Bill to be a sociable fellow.

In all of these Ss of (10), NP$_2$ in the main clause, *Bill,* is mandatory. The main verbs of (10) take both an object and a complement, and, following the rule (9), it is the object of the main verb that serves as subject of the infinitival complement verb.

There are in addition to the verbs listed in (10) a number of verbs which take complements and which take objects only optionally. For example, in (11a), NP$_2$, *Bill,* is optional, so that both (11b) and (11c) are acceptable Ss.

(11) a. John wanted (Bill) to leave.
        NP$_1$    V    (NP$_2$) to inf vb
     b. John wanted Bill to leave.
     c. John wanted to leave.

In such Ss, the subject of the complement verb is NP$_2$ when present, and in its absence, NP$_1$. In (11b) it is *Bill* who is to leave, and in (11c), *John.* A partial list of verbs for which an object is optional is given in (12) and (13). In (12) it is the main clause object *Bill* which serves as complement subject. In (13) it is the main clause subject *John* which serves as complement subject.

(12) a. John wanted Bill to leave.
     b. John begged Bill to leave.
     c. John expected Bill to leave.
     d. John asked Bill to leave.
     e. John liked Bill to be on time.
     f. John preferred Bill to be on time.
     g. John chose Bill to bell the cat.

(13) a. John wanted to leave.
     b. John begged to leave.
     c. John expected to leave.
     d. John asked to leave.
     e. John preferred to be on time.
     f. John liked to be on time.
     g. John chose to bell the cat.

We can characterize the subject assignment for complement verb in these Ss by formulating a general principle that in all these cases, *the implicit subject of the complement verb is the NP most closely preceding it.* We will refer to this principle as the Minimal Distance

Principle, borrowing a term used by Rosenbaum (1965).[2] The Minimal Distance Principle (MDP) holds for the examples above, as well as for other related cases. Consider its application to the Ss of (14) (complement subject indicated by italics).

(14)  a. *John* wanted to leave.
      b. John wanted *Bill* to leave.
      c. John saw *Bill* throw the ball.
      d. John saw *Bill* driving by.
      e. John suspected *Bill* of being a thief.
      f. John told *Bill* what to do.

In all of these cases, the implicit subject of the complement verb is the first NP preceding it. In selecting this NP as subject, a listener operates in accordance with the MDP.

Now, however, consider S (15), which constitutes an exception to the MDP. S (15) has the same surface structure as the Ss of (12), but it differs from them in that the implicit subject of the complement verb is $NP_1$ and not $NP_2$.

(15)  John promised Bill to leave.

In this S it is *John* who intends to leave.[3] To interpret this S correctly, the listener must have learned a special rule connected with *promise* which says

(16)  For a S of the form
      $NP_1$  promise  $NP_2$  to inf vb
      violate the MDP and assign $NP_1$ as subject of the inf vb.

There are very few such constructions in English. It seems to be a characteristic of the verb *promise,* as opposed to the majority of verbs which dominate complements as in (10) and (12), that subject assignment for the complement verb violates the MDP and follows the special rule (16).

There are a number of features of the verb *promise* which may bear on this exceptional syntactic characteristic which it displays. If we consider the verbs in (10) from a semantic viewpoint, we see that many of them are in the nature of commands:

   *tell, order, force, compel, require,* etc.

2. Rosenbaum formulates the Minimal Distance Principle as an erasure principle governing deletion of complement subject in the surface structure of embedded Ss of the sort discussed here (1965, 1967). We will use his terminology as convenient also in discussing the recognition process for such Ss.
3. This exception to the MDP is pointed out by Rosenbaum in *The Grammar of English Predicate Constructions,* Cambridge, Mass.: MIT Press, 1967, p. 68.

*Promise* is in a distinct semantic category from these command verbs. We may say that each semantic class — command verbs on the one hand, and *promise* on the other — has associated with it a separate syntactic process. For the command verbs, the infinitival complement verb relates to the main clause object; for *promise,* it relates to the main clause subject.

| Semantic class | Syntactic process |
|---|---|
| 1. command verbs | 1. complement vb relates to main clause object |
| 2. *promise* | 2. complement vb relates to main clause subject |

Thus we have two semantic classes, and an unambiguous syntactic process associated with each. Now notice that there is in addition a third class of verbs which lies semantically somewhere between a command and a promise. These are verbs like *ask* and *beg* which are in the nature of a request. Interestingly enough, the semantics of *ask* and *beg* permit both syntactic processes to be associated with them. The complement verb may relate either to the main clause object, as in (17), or to the main clause subject, as in (18).

(17)   a. The teacher asked the child to leave the room.
       b. John begged Bill to change the tire.

(18)   a. The child asked the teacher (for permission) to leave the room.
       b. John begged Bill (to be allowed) to change the tire.

Thus we may insert a third semantic class into our above representation, with which both syntactic processes may be associated:

| Semantic class | Syntactic process |
|---|---|
| 1. command verbs | 1. complement vb relates to main clause object |
| 2. request verbs | 2. complement vb relates to main clause subject or object |
| 3. *promise* | 3. complement vb relates to main clause subject |

To approach the difference between *promise* and our other verbs in another way, we may consider the different categories of verbs which introduce indirect speech or quoted speech in the complement clause. If we look at the characteristics of this indirect speech when it is transposed into direct speech, we will notice that for our command verbs, the result is an imperative:

John ordered Mary to move the car.→
"Move the car!"

*Promise,* however, does not have this characteristic. *Promise* is not in the nature of a command, and the indirect speech cannot be transposed into an imperative. Obviously when the direct speech is in the first person it cannot be an imperative:

John promised Mary that he would pay his debts.→
"I will pay my debts."

But even when the direct speech is in the second person, it is not an imperative:

John promised Mary that she would get a bicycle for her birthday.→
"You will get a bicycle for your birthday."

Notice that a verb like *told* exhibits two possibilities for the transposition of the indirect speech into direct speech in the second person. Depending on the structure of the complement, the direct speech may be either in the imperative or not:

Imperative: John told Mary to get a bicycle.→
"Get a bicycle!"
Nonimperative: John told Mary that she would get a bicycle.→
"You will get a bicycle."

*Promise* differs in that it permits only the latter possibility, the nonimperative.

There is another aspect of the verb *promise* which is discussed by Austin (1962), and which may have a bearing on its unusual syntactic characteristics. Austin distinguishes between 'statements' and 'performative utterances,' pointing out that whereas many Ss that a speaker utters state a fact or report something, in other Ss the speaker is actually doing an action by uttering the S. That is, the speaker is not just saying something about an action, but is actually performing the action by uttering the S. Examples of such Ss from Austin (1962) are:

I bet you it will rain tomorrow.
I apologize for the error.
I deny having been there.
I promise you to try harder.

The act of betting, apologizing, denying, and promising is performed by the very utterances of the Ss. Perhaps this aspect of the verb *promise* may provide additional insight into its syntactic non-conformity.

*Promise,* then, constitutes an exception to the MDP, which applies very generally in English. Since the MDP applies so extensively throughout the language, it would seem likely that the child learns this principle, and applies it across the board, so to speak, for a period of time. We hypothesize that this is the case, and will investigate the child's interpretation of Ss in which a correct interpretation requires a violation of the MDP. We expect to find a stage of development in which children have learned the MDP and have not yet learned rule (16). These children should select $NP_2$ as subject of the infinitival complement verb in (19) as well as (20), and report that it is Bill who is supposed to do the work in both cases.

(19)  John promised Bill to shovel the driveway.
(20)  John told Bill to shovel the driveway.

Once rule (16) is learned, the child should distinguish these two cases, and correctly report that in (19) it is John who intends to do the work.

A second verb which signals violation of the MDP is *ask* in constructions of the form

(21) I    asked    him    what    to    do.[4]

$NP_1$    ask    $NP_2$    wh-    to    inf vb

Consider the contrast between (22) and (23):

(22)  I asked him what to do.
(23)  I told him what to do.

The paraphrase of (22) is *I asked him what I should do,* whereas the paraphrase of (23) is *I told him what he should do.* When the subject is omitted from the wh-clause as in (22) and (23), the resulting surface structures are identical, and the task of distinguishing them falls to the listener. He must know to employ the MDP in one case, and to violate it in the other. To do this, the listener must know a special fact about *ask:* that in constructions such as (22), *ask* signals violation of the MDP. He must acquire a rule for *ask* similar to rule (16) for *promise:*

4. Vendler points out this construction as an exception to the general rule of English in *Adjectives and Nominalizations,* The Hague: Mouton & Co., 1968, p. 69.

(24) For a S of the form

$NP_1$ ask $NP_2$ wh- to inf vb

violate the MDP and assign $NP_1$ as subject of the inf vb.

We hypothesize that the child will learn the correct interpretation for (22) later than the correct interpretation for (23). Before he acquires rule (24), we expect that the child will assign to (22) the interpretation

I asked him what he should do.

Once rule (24) is learned, he should correctly assign the interpretation

I asked him what I should do.

(C) A conflict exists between two of the potential syntactic structures associated with a particular verb.

We would like to draw a distinction here between examples (19) and (22) in the preceding section.

(19) John promised Bill to shovel the driveway.

(22) I asked him what to do.

In both of these Ss the Minimal Distance Principle is violated and we have postulated that as a result they will be correctly interpreted by the child later than Ss (20) and (23).

(20) John told Bill to shovel the driveway.

(23) I told him what to do.

We would like now to discuss a difference in the degree of complexity evidenced by Ss (19) and (22), and to show that (22) is considerably more complex than (19).

The difference between these two constructions lies in the nature of the verbs *ask* and *promise*. If we consider the information that a speaker has available when he knows a verb in his language, we see that part of this information concerns the types of structures that may be associated with the verb. That is, a verb may permit, for example, a direct object:

(25) John ate dinner.

Or it may permit complements of various sorts:

(26) John believed Bill to be a thief.

(27) John knew that Bill was hungry.

and so on. The total set of constructions permitted by a verb is part of the information that a speaker has learned and has available in using his language. Fodor, Garrett, and Bever (1968) have advanced the view that this information about the 'lexical character' of the verb is an important factor in sentential complexity. They consider that in interpreting a S, a listener must consider the lexical character of its main verb, and that 'in general, the greater the variety of deep structure configurations the lexicon associates with the main verb of a sentence, the more complicated the sentence should be.'[5] They present experimental evidence to show that increased complexity is evidenced by Ss whose main verbs have a higher number of potential syntactic structures associated with them lexically.

We would like to add to this view, and consider that it is not just the *number* of potential syntactic structures associated with a verb lexically that contributes to complexity, but also the nature of these structures with respect to one another. If two different structures associated with the same verb happen to require conflicting rules for their analyses, then the degree of complexity will be considerably increased. The verb *ask* is a case in point, with respect to the MDP described above.

Consider the example dealt with above:

(28)  John asked Bill what to do.

We said that in order to learn to interpret this S, the child must acquire a special rule which says, 'In the case of *ask + wh- + to + inf vb,* violate the MDP.' But notice that *ask* also permits the structure

(29)  John asked Bill to leave.

which follows the MDP, i.e., it is Bill who is to leave. To interpret this S, the child must follow the rule: 'In the case of *ask + to + inf vb,* follow the MDP.' Thus the final system which the child must acquire must contain two opposing rules for *ask:*

(30)  For *ask + to + inf vb,* follow the MDP.
(31)  For *ask + wh- + to + inf vb,* violate the MDP.

The task of acquiring two contradictory rules for the same verb certainly poses a problem of considerable difficulty.

The notion of 'same verb' must be analyzed further. Notice that *ask* is used in two different senses in (30) and (31). Ss exemplifying these two constructions are (32) and (33).

5. Fodor, Garrett, and Bever, "Some Syntactic Determinants of Sentential Complexity, II: Verb Structure," *Perception and Psychophysics,* 3 (1968), p. 454.

(32) John asked Bill to leave.
(33) John asked Bill what to do.

In (32) *ask* is used in the sense of *request* ($ask_r$), and in (33) it is used in the sense of *question* ($ask_q$). In other languages, these two verbs are distinguished lexically. In German, $ask_r$ is *bitten,* and $ask_q$ is *fragen.* In Russian, $ask_r$ is *poprosit',* and $ask_q$ is *sprosit'.* Since English has only one lexical item for these two senses of *ask,* the syntactic complexity of the word and its associated structures is increased.

The analysis of *ask* is further complicated by the fact that (32) has a second less likely interpretation, namely

(34) John asked Bill (for permission) to leave.

in which *John* is the subject of *leave.* This ambiguity was pointed out in §2(B) in our discussion of the three semantic classes of verbs with which we are dealing:

| Semantic class | Syntactic process |
|---|---|
| 1. command verbs | 1. complement vb relates to main clause object |
| 2. request verbs | 2. complement vb relates to main clause subject *or* object |
| 3. *promise, ask*$_q$ | 3. complement vb relates to main clause subject |

$Ask_r$ as in (32) belongs in class 2, and has both syntactic processes associated with it. $Ask_r$ is therefore inconsistent both within itself and with respect to $ask_q$, which belongs in class 3 along with *promise.*

Considering these various complications pertaining to *ask,* we propose three levels of complexity with regard to the application of the MDP.

**Table 2.1.** Three Levels of Complexity with Regard to MDP Application

| Complement construction | Rule for MDP application |
|---|---|
| 1. *Normal pattern* | |
|   a. John told Bill to leave. | APPLY MDP, SUBJ = NP$_2$ |
|   b. John asked$_1$ Bill to leave. | |
| 2. *Consistent exception* | |
|   c. John promised Bill to leave. | VIOLATE MDP, SUBJ = NP$_1$ |
| 3. *Inconsistent exception* | |
|   d. John asked$_2$ Bill what to do. | VIOLATE MDP, SUBJ = NP$_1$ |
|   e. John asked$_3$ Bill (for permission) to leave. | |

The important constructions to note here are Ss (b), (d), and (e), with *ask* labeled ask$_1$, ask$_2$, and ask$_3$. We expect that the inconsistency between ask$_1$ on the one hand, and ask$_2$ and ask$_3$ on the other, will cause children difficulty in learning ask$_2$ and ask$_3$. We hypothesize that Ss (a) and (b), which exhibit the normal pattern, will be learned first; that (c) will be learned second; and that (d) and (e) will be learned last. For *promise* the child must learn to violate the MDP, but at least *promise* is consistent within itself.[6] For *ask* he must learn the rather curious property: Keep the MDP, but violate it some of the time. We expect this difficulty to result in relatively late acquisition of the conditions of violation.

(D) Restrictions on a grammatical operation apply under certain limited conditions only.

Under this heading we would like to deal with an aspect of the general question of pronominalization, and the information used by the listener who must make decisions about the reference of pronouns in the Ss that he hears. In many ways the problem is an extremely complicated one, as shown by Ross (1967) in his detailed treatment of pronominalization. If we consider some Ss which contain both a pronoun and an NP, we see that in many cases the pronoun may refer to the NP which is present elsewhere in the S:

(35)  a.  John knew that he was going to win the race.
      b.  When he was tired, John usually took a nap.
      c.  After John took a drink, he felt better.
      d.  Knowing that he was going to be late bothered John.
      e.  John expected Mary to like him.
      f.  John's mother was disappointed in him.

In all of these Ss, the pronoun *he* or *him* may refer to *John,* i.e., identity of the pronoun with the occurring NP is possible. However, this identity is not required in the Ss of (35). The pronouns in (35) may also refer to someone else not mentioned in the S. The structure of the S does not impose a restriction on the pronoun's reference,

6. *Promise* also has the characteristic that it can be followed by a direct object plus complement clause, in which case the complement verb refers to the direct object. In the S *They promised him a secretary to type his letters.* it is the secretary who will do the typing. If the indirect object *him* is omitted from this S, the resulting S is ambiguous. In *They promised a secretary to type his letters.* the subject of *type* is either *they* or *secretary,* depending on whether *secretary* is considered to be the indirect object or the direct object of *promise*. We are indebted to Karl V. Teeter for pointing out this feature of the verb *promise*.

but permits the pronoun either an identity or a nonidentity relationship with the occurring NP. Factors other than structure may be present which influence the pronoun's interpretation in a given S, such as semantic effect, or stress placement. For example, in (35b),

When he was tired, John usually took a nap.

the most likely interpretation is that *he* refers to *John,* but it can also refer to someone else, in the spirit of

(36)  When the mother feels cold, the child puts on a sweater.

In (35c) and (35d),

After John took a drink, he felt better.
Knowing that he was going to be late bothered John.

the most likely interpretation again is that *he* refers to *John,* but if the pronoun is contrastively stressed, the nonidentity interpretation becomes the more likely one. The Ss of (35), then, do not restrict pronominal reference by their structure, but exhibit both possibilities of reference.

There are cases, however, in which the structure of the S does restrict the pronoun's reference. In (37) the pronoun cannot refer to *John,* but must refer to someone else outside the S:

(37)  a.  He knew that John was going to win the race.
      b.  He expected Mary to like John.
      c.  Knowing that John was going to win the race bothered him.

Nonidentity is required in these constructions, as opposed to the constructions of (35). Restriction of pronominal reference to nonidentity is apparently the only type of structural restriction which occurs in English. We do not find Ss in which the pronoun's reference is restricted on the basis of structure to an identity relationship.

It is difficult to characterize the conditions under which this restriction applies, i.e., under which nonidentity of pronoun with NP is required. Ross (1967) treats this question in detail, and indicates that a satisfactory account covering all occurrences still remains to be worked out. For our purposes here, we do not wish to enter into a discussion of these complexities, but merely to point out that they have been discussed in the literature, and have served as our motivation for exploring the question of pronominal reference in children's grammar. Since the eventual system of rules for nonidentity that a speaker must acquire is fairly complex, we might expect that the child accomplishes the task relatively late. We wish to confine ourselves in this study to a much simpler question than that of the whole system of restrictive rules for nonidentity that the mature speaker commands. We wish to investigate only a very elementary question concerning the onset of this acquisition, namely, at what stage of development the child becomes aware that a nonidentity restriction on pronominal reference exists in his language at all. A common and simple construction exhibiting this restriction is the one illustrated in (37a):

He knew that John was going to win the race.

We will attempt to determine, for children of different ages, whether they recognize that in (37a) the pronoun cannot refer to *John,* whereas in Ss like (38), the pronoun may refer to *John.*

(38) a.  If he wins the race, John will be happy.
b.  John knew that he was going to win the race.

To do this they must be aware, first, of the notion of nonidentity restriction on pronominal reference, and second, they must know to apply this restriction selectively, to (37a) and not to (38). The underlying principles governing this selectivity are not completely understood, but roughly we can say that a pronoun which precedes the NP in a S, (37a) and (38a), is restricted to nonidentity when in a main clause (37a), but not when in a subordinate clause (38a). For a more specific statement, and an account of exceptions, see Ross (1967).

We hypothesize that children who have not yet learned to apply the nonidentity requirement to constructions such as (37a) will interpret Ss of this form as if the pronoun has unrestricted reference, and report for some such Ss the interpretation

(39)  John knew that John was going to win the race.

Once a child has learned that a nonidentity requirement applies to Ss of this construction, he should report only the interpretation

(40)  Somebody else knew that John was going to win the race.

At both stages we expect the child to interpret Ss of the form of (38) with unrestricted pronominal reference.

# 3 Experimental Design

## 3.1. Children in the Sample

Our sample consisted of forty children, eight each from kindergarten through fourth grade. We did the interviewing at the Davis Elementary School in Newton, Massachusetts. Davis is a predominantly middle-class school, which has, nevertheless, some children from widely varying socioeconomic backgrounds. We told the teacher in each class that we were interested in a cross section of children in terms of background and ability, and requested that she choose four average children, two above average, and two below, insofar as possible from a variety of socioeconomic backgrounds. The children's ages ranged from 5 to 10 years. There were 22 boys and 18 girls in the sample.

## 3.2. Interview Procedures

The children were interviewed by the author over a three-month period, from November 1967 to January 1968. We visited the school one morning a week, seeing about five children, individually, at each visit. Each interview lasted about a half-hour, with the constructions presented in the following order:

1. ask/tell   (15 minutes)
2. promise/tell   (5 minutes)
3. easy to see   (1 minute)
4. pronominalization   (10 minutes)

The *ask/tell* set of questions required the presence of a second child to serve as a conversational partner for the child being interviewed. These questions were therefore presented first, and the child who had just completed his interview was asked to remain during this first portion of the next interview. This particular technique of having the 'experienced' child on hand to introduce the new subject and remain with him for a while turned out to be beneficial all around. The younger children tended to come in unnaturally quiet and somewhat apprehensive about what was going to happen, and the presence of a classmate who had already been through it all was very reassuring. It broke the ice and made for more natural conversation until things got going on their own. The older children were far more confident, but even with them it was helpful to have the second child present. It lent spirit and an atmosphere of anticipation to have a friend bring you in who assured you it had been 'cool,' who kidded around, and who was an old hand at all this questioning. And it provided a sense of play during the interview itself to have two children there who, as it turned out, were having a good time together. The second child left toward the end of the *ask/tell* questions (during the third interview sequence, see p. 51), and the relatively short *promise* and *easy to see* questions were presented next. The pronominalization interview was a long one (ten minutes) and was kept till last so that it could be postponed until the next visit if a child became tired. Some of the kindergarten children did tire noticeably after 20 minutes of questioning, and they were given the pronominalization test separately the following week.

The interviews were tape recorded for later transcription, and some notes were taken during the interviews. We kept note-taking to a minimum, marking down interesting observations when warranted and if it did not interrupt the course of the questioning.

A second set of *ask/tell* questions (described at the end of §4(C)) was run with different children at two other schools. For this second run we interviewed fifteen children, five each from grades 1, 2, and 3. Grade 1 was run at the Parmenter School in Arlington, Massachusetts, and grades 2 and 3 at the Bridge School in Lexington, Massachusetts. These two schools are also middle-class schools, and in this case we asked the teacher to select average children. These short interviews were completed in one morning at each of the schools.

### 3.3. Design of Test Sentences

Before presenting the test Ss and discussing the interviews with the children, we would like to indicate the thinking that went into the choice of the test Ss and the design of the interview situation. Our purpose was to test the child's knowledge of syntactic structures by investigating his ability to interpret Ss exhibiting these structures. In order to judge his knowledge of a syntactic structure, it is necessary to present this structure to him in as neutral a context as possible. That is, we must remove semantic and situational cues which provide him with clues about the S's correct interpretation. In the absence of clues of this sort relating to factors other than structure, his interpretations will reflect his knowledge of the structure itself. For example, consider our S

(41)  John is easy to see.

This S was selected because the meanings of the words permit two analyses that make sense. It can be easy both for John to see, and for others to see John. In order to assign the correct interpretation, the child must utilize knowledge about the structure of this S. If he has not yet acquired this knowledge, i.e., learned this structure, he will be unable to assign the correct interpretation. He will assign instead the relatively simpler one which he has learned to assign to other Ss exhibiting this same surface structure. This is not to say that the child is unable at this stage of development to understand, with the aid of situational or semantic cues, innumerable other Ss which have this same structure. The fact that he understands perfectly well Ss such as

(42)  The book is hard to read.
(43)  These steps are easy to climb.

does not imply that he is utilizing knowledge of structure. The meanings of the words in these two Ss do not permit any other analysis that makes sense. Books do not read, and steps do not climb. It can be only that people read books and that people climb steps. Indeed, given just the words *book — hard — read*, or *steps — easy — climb*, with no structure at all, the only way to make sense out of them is to assign what we have been calling the more difficult interpretation. The fact that the child can do this in the semantically unambiguous case does not tell us whether he knows the structure. To find this out, we have to see what he does in the semantically 'ambiguous' case where two different combinations of the words both make sense.

This, then, was our procedure: to select Ss that exhibit the test syntactic structures with no contextual or semantic clues to influence the child's interpretations. His only basis for correct interpretation is his knowledge of structure.

# 4 Experiments

We will now discuss the tests that we gave to the children, and describe the interview sessions and the results that they yielded. We will discuss separately each of the constructions, and then correlate the results in Chapter 5.

The constructions are discussed here in the same order as in Chapter 2: (A) Easy to see; (B) Promise; (C) Ask/Tell; (D) Pronominalization. A sample interview sheet and a photograph showing the toys used are presented at the beginning of each subsection.

## 4.1. Easy to See

**Interview**

*Initial setting up:* Place on the table in front of the child a blindfolded doll.

*Interview:*
1. Is this doll easy to see or hard to see?
2. Would you make her easy/hard to see.

(Choice of *easy/hard* in question 2 determined by child's response to first question)

3. (For child who answers *Hard to see*)
   Why was she hard to see in the beginning?
   What did you do to make her easier to see?
   Why did that make her easier to see?

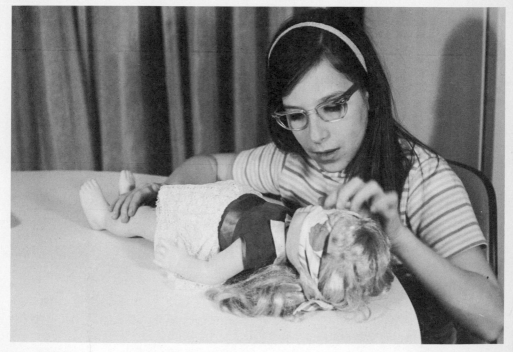

**Figure 4.1.** *Easy to see* Experiment. Question: Is this doll easy to see or hard to see?

## Discussion

*Test construction:* (A) *John is easy to see.*

*Nature of complexity:* The true grammatical relations which hold among the words in a S are not expressed directly in its surface structure.

In this interview, the children's interpretation of the S form

　　(44)　John is easy to see.

is tested. We have shown in §2(A) that for the two Ss of identical surface structure (45) and (46)

(45)  John is eager to see.
(46)  John is easy to see.

the underlying grammatical relations are expressed more directly in the surface structure of (45) than in (46). Accordingly we postulated that a child will pass through a stage of development in which he will interpret (45) correctly more readily than (46). We expect that during this period he will, in the absence of situational and semantic cues, tend to assign a (45) interpretation to S (46). Once he has fully mastered the rules applying to S (46), he should correctly assign the (46) interpretation where required.

We wished to design a test in which situational and semantic cues would be removed insofar as possible, so that the child would be forced to select an interpretation relying on his knowledge of syntactic structure alone. We selected the S

(47)  The doll is easy to see.

which can be interpreted as (46) (correctly) to mean that someone else sees the doll, or as (45) (incorrectly) to mean that the doll is doing the seeing, i.e., that it is easy for the doll to see. What we did was to question the child about a blindfolded doll, and asked

Is this doll easy to see or hard to see?

The child who incorrectly assigned a (45) interpretation answered HARD TO SEE, and the child who correctly assigned a (46) interpretation answered EASY TO SEE. Depending on the child's answer, different questions were then put to him. The child who incorrectly answered HARD TO SEE was asked:

Would you make her easy to see.
Why was she hard to see in the beginning?
What did you do to her to make her easier to see?
Why did that make her easier to see?

The child who correctly answered EASY TO SEE was asked:

Would you make her hard to see.

Further questions were asked of this second group of children only when their answers left some doubt as to their interpretation of the test question. When this doubt existed, they were questioned as the former group.

We would like to point out here that the interview was carried out fairly casually and in a conversational manner. We did not stick rigidly to the questions listed above, but rather explored the child's interpretation in a number of different ways, depending on the answers we were getting. The one restriction that we held to was to keep the first two questions basically the same for each child:

Is this doll easy to see or hard to see?
Would you make her easy/hard to see.

But beyond this, additional questioning depended a good bit on the reactions of the child. The examples which will be presented below illustrate this.

The results show that, much as expected, the younger children in general answered incorrectly, and the older children answered correctly. The number of wrong answers dropped with increase in age. At the extremes, almost all 5-year-olds answered incorretly, and all the 9-year-olds answered correctly. The 6s, 7s, and 8s were mixed. The results are shown in Table 4.1.

**Table 4.1.** Children Who Give Correct and Incorrect Interpretations to the Question *Is this doll easy to see or hard to see?* when Shown a Blindfolded Doll. Ages are given in years and months (5.2 = 5 years, 2 months). A prime (5.3′) distinguishes different children of the same age.

| Correct Interpretation Answer: *Easy to see* 26 children | | Incorrect Interpretation Answer: *Hard to see* 14 children | |
|---|---|---|---|
| boys | girls | boys | girls |
| 5.2′ | 6.5′ | 5.0 | 5.1′ |
| 5.10 | 6.9′ | 5.1 | 5.3 |
| 6.7 | 7.0 | 5.2 | 6.5 |
| 7.3 | 7.0′ | 5.3′ | 6.6 |
| 7.9 | 7.1 | 5.3″ | |
| 8.4 | 7.2 | 6.9 | |
| 8.8 | 8.6 | 6.10 | |
| 9.2 | 8.7 | 7.6 | |
| 9.7′ | 8.8′ | 8.2 | |
| 9.7″ | 8.10 | 8.5 | |
| 9.8 | 9.1 | | |
| 9.9 | 9.7 | | |
| | 9.8′ | | |
| | 10.0 | | |

For the children who said that the doll was HARD TO SEE, every one without exception responded to the instruction

Would you make her easy to see.

by removing the blindfold. When asked why she was hard to see in the beginning, they said it was because she had a blindfold on, or because her eyes were covered. When asked to explain what they did, they said simply that they took off the blindfold so she could see. Following are a number of samples of the conversations. The children's responses are *italicized* and indented. Descriptive comments appear in parentheses.

*Eric H., 5.2* (5 years, 2 months)
Is this doll easy to see or hard to see?
    *Hard to see*
Will you make her easy to see.
    *Ok* (He removes blindfold)
Will you explain what you did.
    *Took off this* (Pointing to blindfold)
And why did that make her easier to see?
    *So she can see*

*Scotty G., 5.0*
Is this doll easy to see or hard to see?
    *Hard to see*
Could you make her easy to see.
    (Pause)
Is there a way you could make her easier to see?
    *Yeah, you can untie that*
Why is she easy to see now?
    *'Cause I took this off*
When she was hard to see, who couldn't see?
    (He points to doll)
Her?
    *Yeah*
And now that she's easy to see, who's doing the seeing?
    *She is*
And she's easy to see. Could you tell me that? *She's easy to see.* Can you say that?
    *She* is *easy to see*

*Chris L., 5.1*
Can you tell me if this doll is hard to see or easy to see.
    *Hard to see*
Could you make her easy to see.
    (He removes blindfold)
Why was she hard to see?
    *This is over*
And what did you do to make her easy to see?
    *Take it off*
(I replaced the blindfold at this point.)
Can you tell me now . . . can you just say, *The doll is hard to see.*
    *Hard to see*
(I removed the blindfold.)
Ok. Now what is she?
    *Can see*
Hm?
    *She can see*
That's right. Did she get easy to see? Can you say, *She's easy to see.*
    *She's easy to see*
Who's doing the seeing?
    *This* (Pointing to blindfold)
What was this doing?
    *Going off her*
And what did it make her when it got off her?
    *Like that*
Yes. So now she's easy to see?
    *Yep*
What does she see?
    *Up there*


*Christine M., 5.1'*
Here's Chatty Cathy. Can you tell me whether she's easy to see or hard to see.
    *Hard*
Could you make her easy to see?
    (Removes blindfold)
Can you tell me why she was hard to see in the beginning?
    *'Cause she had this over her eyes*

'Cause she had the blindfold on. And what did you do? Explain what you did.
> *Take it off*

And what did that make her?
> *Uh . . .*

Did that make her easy to see?
> *Yes*

Can you say that? Say, *I took the blindfold off*
> *I took the blindfold off her*

And it made her . . .
> *See*


*Lisa V., 6.5*

Is this doll easy to see or hard to see?
> *Hard to see*

Will you make her easy to see.
> *If I can get this untied*

Will you explain why she was hard to see.
> (To doll): *Because you had a blindfold over your eyes*

And what did you do?
> *I took it off*


*Jimmy H., 6.10*

Is this doll easy to see or hard to see?
> *Hard to see*

Will you please make her easier to see.
> (Removes blindfold)

Can you explain why she was hard to see in the beginning.
> (Silence)

Well, what did you do that made her easier to see?
> *Take the blindfold thing off — cloth off*


*Peter F., 6.9*

Is this doll easy to see or hard to see?
> *Hard to see*

Why?
> *'Cause she got a blindfold*

Will you make her easy to see.
> (Removes blindfold)

Will you explain what you did.
> *I punched her*
> (An accurate description)

How did that make her easier to see?
*It punched off the blindfold*

The children who correctly answered that the doll was *Easy to see* responded to the instruction

Would you make her hard to see.

with a number of different tactics. Some children hid the doll under the table, others put something on top of her or turned her over, and others merely closed or covered their own eyes. In most cases it was clear that they interpreted the question correctly, and no further discussion was necessary.

Following are sample interviews with the children who interpreted the question correctly.

*Ann C., 8.8*
Here's Chatty Cathy. Can you tell me, is she easy to see or hard to see?
*Easy*
Could you make her hard to see? Can you think of a way?
*In the dark*

*Ann M., 8.7*
This is Chatty Cathy. Is she easy to see or hard to see?
*Easy*
Would you make her hard to see.
*So you can't see her at all?*
Ok.
(Places doll under table)
Tell what you did.
*I put her under the table.*

*Julianne S., 7.2*
Here's Chatty Cathy. Is she easy to see or hard to see?
*Hard to see her eyes*
Yes. And the rest of her?
*Easy*

What is noteworthy here is that there are children up to the age of 8 who are still assigning the wrong interpretation to this construction. In our sample of forty, the three children over 7 who did so were boys. Given the small size of the sample, we do not attach any particular significance to this sex division. In the preliminary questioning with other children that we carried out while devising the eventual interview techniques, we did find girls beyond 7 who responded incorrectly. One notable case was an 8-year-old girl who went so far as to misuse the construction in her own speech during our conversation. We asked her to tell who is doing the pleasing in the S *John is easy to please.* She said *John* is, and we asked her to elaborate a bit. Well, she said, he's probably very obedient and it's not hard for him to do what he's supposed to do. We asked her who he is easy to please, and she said, "He's easy to please his mother, probably."

The fact that there are children of 7 and 8 who have not yet mastered this construction indicates that fairly basic syntactic learning is still going on considerably beyond the age at which it is generally considered to be complete. By removing the semantic clues which are normally present in most of what the children hear, we were able to question their knowledge of the syntax alone. Similar gaps in syntactic knowledge were revealed by the other constructions that we tested as well, and will be presented in succeeding sections.

## 4.2. Promise

**Interview**

*Initial setting up*: Place on the table in front of the child a book, and the figures of Donald Duck and Bozo.

*Interview*:
1. *Establish that the child knows the meaning of* promise.
   Can you tell me what you would say to your friend if you promise him that you'll call him up this afternoon. How would you say that to him? What would you say to him?
   What do you mean when you make somebody a promise?
   What's special about a promise?
2. *Have the child identify the dolls.*
   Can you tell me who this is? (Indicate Donald Duck)
   And this? (Indicate Bozo)
3. *Have the child practice the actions.*
   Now, I want you to make them do some things, and I'll tell you what.
   Ok?
   Will you show me Donald doing a somersault.
   Make Bozo hop up and down.

Have Bozo lie down.
Make Donald stand on the book.

4. *Practice sentences.*
 Bozo wants to do a somersault. Make him do it.
 Bozo wants Donald to do a somersault. Make him do it.
 Donald decides to stand on the book. Make him do it.
 Donald says he's going to lie down. Have him do it.

5. *Test sentences.*
 Bozo tells Donald to hop up and down. Make him hop.
 Bozo promises Donald to do a somersault. Make him do it.
 Donald promises Bozo to hop up and down. Make him hop.
 Bozo tells Donald to lie down. Make him do it.
 Bozo promises Donald to stand on the book. Make him do it.
 Donald promises Bozo to lie down. Have him lie down.
 Bozo tells Donald to do a somersault. Make him do it.
 Donald promises Bozo to stand on the book. Make him do it.

**Discussion**

*Test construction:* (B) *John promised Bill to go.*

*Nature of complexity:* The syntactic structure assocated with a particular word is at variance with a general pattern in the language.

In this interview the children's knowledge of a particular syntactic structure associated with the word *promise* is examined. We have seen above that *promise* is an exception to a general pattern in English in that in a S such as

(48)  John promised Bill to shovel the driveway.

the underlying subject of the complement verb *shovel* is *John,* not *Bill.* The general pattern of English is exemplified by a S such as

(49)  John told Bill to shovel the driveway.

in which the underlying subject of the complement verb *shovel* is *Bill.* It appears to be an unusual characteristic of *promise* that in the construction

$$NP_1 \quad promise \quad NP_2 \quad to \quad inf \ vb$$

$NP_1$ rather than $NP_2$ serves as subject of the infinitival complement verb. We hypothesized that children will assign the wrong subject in Ss such as (48) until such time as they learn this special structure associated with *promise.*

The test situation consisted of having the child manipulate two

**Figure 4.2.** *Promise* Experiment. Instruction: Bozo promises Donald to stand on the book. Make him do it.

dolls, Bozo and Donald Duck, according to instruction. We presented the child with the following set of Ss containing *promise* and *tell,* and asked him to show the correct doll performing for each one.

> Bozo tells Donald to hop up and down. Make him hop.
> Bozo promises Donald to do a somersault. Make him do it.
> Donald promises Bozo to hop up and down. Make him hop.
> Bozo tells Donald to lie down. Make him do it.
> Bozo promises Donald to stand on the book. Make him do it.
> Donald promises Bozo to lie down. Have him lie down.

Bozo tells Donald to do a somersault. Make him do it.
Donald promises Bozo to stand on the book. Make him do it.

These Ss were designed to contain no semantic clues which would aid the child in assigning a subject to the complement verb. In each case, both Donald and Bozo can equally well perform the indicated action. The child's choice, then, must depend on his knowledge of the verbs *promise* and *tell,* and the structures which are associated with them.

The complete interview is presented at the beginning of this section. We will discuss it step by step here

Prior to presenting the test Ss to the child, we carried out the following steps. First we checked to see that he knew the meaning of the word *promise*. We asked him if he knew what a promise was, and could explain it, or if he had ever promised anybody anything and could tell what, or if he could tell what he might say to his friend if he wants to promise him that he'll call him up this afternoon, or that he'll come over and play this afternoon. "You want to promise your friend that you'll call him up this afternoon. What would you say?" One or another of these questions succeeded with each child, and in fact everyone knew what a promise is. This was considered a prerequisite for administering the test.

Following are samples of the children's answers to this preliminary questioning. These examples are taken from children who subsequently failed the *promise* test, i.e., assigned NP$_2$ as subject in the *promise* Ss as well as the *tell* Ss. These children show that they do in fact know what a promise is, although they have not yet learned the particular test structure associated with it.

*Scotty G., 5.0*
What do you do when you promise somebody something?
  *When you don't fool*

*Jimmy H., 6.10*
You're walking home from school with your friend, and as you're saying goodbye you promise him that you'll call him up this afternoon. How would you say that?
  *I'll call you right up after lunch.*

*Lynn D., 8.10*
Can you tell me what a promise is?
  *It's something that you . . . ah . . .*

Well, how do you promise somebody something? What do you say?

> *I promise I'll give you something for Christmas*

And what do you mean?

> *You mean that you have to give something to him, or do something*

The children's knowledge of the word *tell* had been demonstrated by a preceding test involving *ask* and *tell* and it was not necessary to check it again here.

Second, we asked the child to give the names of the two dolls. Most children identified Donald Duck and Bozo with no trouble. When there was some question, we straightened it out before proceeding. The only confusion that occurred was that some children at first said Mickey Mouse for Donald Duck. There was no problem of confusion between the two figures.

Third, we explained to the child that he was going to make Donald and Bozo do some things, and proceeded with some practice Ss to familiarize him both with the particular actions involved, and also with the specific form of the Ss. As to the actions, the child was told:

> Will you show me Donald doing a somersault.
> Make Bozo hop up and down.
> Have Bozo lie down.
> Make Donald stand on the book.

The children were able to do these things easily. If there was any problem, we simply showed the child what we meant and he reproduced the action. As to the form of the test Ss, they are in two parts, first the S itself, and then a short command.

> Donald tells Bozo to lie down. Make him do it.
> Donald promises Bozo to lie down. Have him do it.

The subject of the S is either giving directions (Donald tells Bozo) or stating an intention (Donald promises Bozo). This format and 'intentional' character of the test Ss was introduced in several practice Ss which the child was asked to do next. If he had any trouble, we discussed the S and repeated it until he was able to do it correctly.

> Bozo wants to do a somersault. Make him do it.
> Bozo wants Donald to do a somersault. Make him do it.
> Donald decides to stand on the book. Make him do it.
> Donald says he's going to lie down. Have him do it.

Finally we presented the test Ss listed earlier. Generally we read the S once and the child chose a figure and performed the action. If a child requested a repetition of a S, or hesitated and looked confused, we repeated the S as many times as he wished. Sometimes after hearing a S, a child would ask "Which one?" To this we answered, "I'll read it again and you see if you can figure it out."

The results are given in Table 4.2. Twenty-one of the forty children

**Table 4.2.** Children's Interpretations of Test Constructions with *promise* and *tell*. The chart shows the children's assignment of subject to complement verb following *promise/tell* in 8 constructions of the type
Donald   Duck   promises/tells   Bozo   to   do   a   somersault.
$NP_1$                 pr/tell              $NP_2$    to inf vb        . . .
Incorrect interpretations (stages 1, 2, 3) assign wrong subjects as indicated. Correct interpretation (stage 4) assigns $NP_2$ following *tell*, $NP_1$ following *promise*.

|  |  |  |
|---|---|---|
|  | Stage 1. | 10 children |
|  | *tell* — all correct | |
|  | *promise* — all wrong | |
|  | Assigned $NP_2$ as subject throughout. | |
|  | Boys: 5.0, 5.1, 5.3′, 6.10, 7.6 | |
|  | Girls: 6.5, 6.6, 7.1, 8.7, 8.10 | |
|  | Stage 2. | 4 children |
|  | *tell* — mixed | |
|  | *promise* — mixed | |
| Incorrect | Assigned both $NP_1$ and $NP_2$ as subject following both | |
| Interpretations | words. | |
|  | Boys: 6.9 | |
|  | Girls: 5.1′, 5.3, 6.9′ | |
|  | Stage 3. | 5 children |
|  | *tell* — all correct | |
|  | *promise* — mixed | |
|  | Assigned $NP_2$ as subject consistently following *tell* | |
|  | and both $NP_1$ and $NP_2$ following *promise*. | |
|  | Boys: 8.2, 9.2, 9.7′ | |
|  | Girls: 6.5′, 8.8′ | |
|  | Stage 4. | 21 children |
|  | *tell* — all correct | |
|  | *promise* — all correct | |
| Correct | Assigned $NP_2$ as subject following *tell*, and $NP_1$ fol- | |
| Interpretation | lowing *promise*. | |
|  | Boys: 5.2, 5.2′, 5.3″, 5.10, 6.7, 7.3, 7.9, 8.4, 8.5, 8.8, 9.7″, 9.8, 9.9 | |
|  | Girls: 7.0, 7.0′, 7.2, 8.6, 9.1, 9.7, 9.8′, 10.0 | |

succeeded in consistently assigning the correct subject to the complement verbs following both *promise* and *tell,* or in other words got
everything right (stage 4). Of the nineteen who made mistakes, ten
were consistent and got every *tell* right and every *promise* wrong
(stage 1). The other nine were inconsistent in their responses: four
had mixed responses to both words (stage 2), five had mixed
responses to *promise* only, getting all *tell* right (stage 3).

We have tentatively ordered these four response categories as
stages 1–4 because we think that this order is indicative of stages of
development. The children's interpretations can be clarified if we
consider the following description as a possible account of their development. In the earliest stage, (1), the child has learned the Minimal Distance Principle described in §2(B), which works for almost
all verbs, and has not yet become aware of this exception to it. His
system for dealing with verbs is uniform: he assigns $NP_2$ as complement subject consistently following both test verbs. Next, the child becomes aware that the MDP sometimes does not apply, and the uniformity he formerly exhibited breaks down. *Promise* is the nonconforming verb, and he violates the MDP for *promise* haphazardly, not
having become sufficiently experienced to control its application and
nonapplication correctly. He is in a transitional phase of acquiring
a new rule for a nonconforming verb which interferes with his pre-
viously uniform system. At first his uncertainty is high, and he even
makes mistakes with a conforming verb (*tell*) in the confusion of
being presented with a sequence of Ss containing both verbs in an
artificial test situation. This is stage (2). Somewhat later (stage 3),
his uncertainty is reduced, and he gets the conforming verb *tell* consistently right, while still exhibiting lack of consistency with the nonconforming verb *promise*. Finally he gains complete control over his
new rule for *promise,* and applies it consistently (stage 4).

It is interesting to note that success in this test is so little dependent
on age. The range for children who get everything right is from 5.2 to
10.0. The range for children in the earliest stage (consistent $NP_2$
assignment) is from 5.0 to 8.10. The 'transitional' children range
from 5.1 to 9.7. It is surprising that the acquisition of this particular
structure is taking place in some children before the age of 5, and in
others after the age of 9. We would like to correlate this development with other aspects of their linguistic development, and will attempt to do so in our final discussion section.

Some of the responses of the children during the interview were
interesting, and we would like to present them here. The preliminary
conversation, in which we tried to establish that the child knew the

meaning of *promise,* yielded some interesting exchanges. Ordinarily we used the S form in which the subject of the complement verb was specified in this initial conversation:

> What would you say if you want to promise your friend that you'll call him up this afternoon?

> How would you promise your friend that you'll come over and play this afternoon? What would you say to him?

However, sometimes we inadvertently used a complement verb without subject:

> If you want to promise your friend to come over and play this afternoon, what would you say to him?

It was in response to these unintentional complements without subject that the children revealed their understanding of the structure verbally, in support of their subsequent actions in manipulating the dolls. For example, Joe M., 5.3, who is in stage (1) above:

> *Joe M., 5.3*
> If you were going to promise your friend to come over and play this afternoon, how would you say that? What would you say?
> *I'd say come over and play with me*
> If you promise your teacher that you'll listen carefully, what would you say to your teacher?
> *I'd say I will*

The next child, also in stage (1) above, produced a sequence of wrong subject assignments, including one where the correct subject was in fact supplied in the question. His response to the first question, in spite of the phrase *to his house,* was so unexpected that we pursued the matter further as follows:

> *Chris L., 5.1*
> If you promise your friend to come over and play this afternoon, to go to his house, what would you say to him?
> *Will you come over?*
> Suppose you promise your mother to be home before dark. What would you say to your mother?
> *Will you be home before dark?*
> Suppose you promise your teacher that you'll listen very carefully, what would you say to your teacher?
> *Listen very carefully*

Can you make a whole sentence out of that? What would you say to your teacher if you want to promise her that you'll listen very carefully?

(Silence)

How about if you promise your friend that you'll go to the movies with him on Saturday afternoon?

*I'll go with him*

The next child, in stage (2) above, displayed the obliging characteristic of speaking out loud for the dolls while carrying out the actions. This provided excellent confirmation of his actions as valid indicators of his S interpretations. Notice that his first answer in the preliminary questioning is correct (1 →), where he is aided by the pronoun *him* in the complement *to call him up*. In contrast, notice his misinterpretation of the second test S (2 →).

> *Peter F., 6.9*
> Preliminary questioning:
> Can you tell me what you would say to your friend if you promise him to call him up this afternoon?
>
> 1 →    *I would . . . and you mean, and I didn't call him up?*
> No. You were walking home from school, and as you leave him you promise him you'll call him up later, when you get home. What would you say?
>
> *I would say I'll call you up this afternoon*
> Test sentences:
> Donald tells Bozo to hop across the table. Can you make him hop? (making Bozo hop) *Bozo, hop across the table*
> Bozo promises Donald to do a somersault. Can you make him do it?
>
> 2 →    (making Donald do the somersault) *I promised you you can do a tumblesault*
> Would you say that again?
>
> *I promised you you could do a tumblesault*

We would like to stress once more here the distinction between knowing the meaning or concept of a word, and knowing the syntactic structures associated with it. Complete knowledge of a word includes both the concept and all the syntactic structures associated with it. The semantics of a word may exclude certain structures, as, for example, *promise* excludes an associated imperative. Every child tested knew the concept of *promise* and at least some of the syntactic structures associated with the word, but only half of the children knew the test structure. One quarter of the children showed no knowledge of it at all, and another quarter evidenced partial command. We see that the process of learning a word may be a lengthy one, which the child may go through fairly slowly. He may acquire the concept of a word and some of its associated structures, and may wait several years before learning an additional associated structure, particularly if it is a problematic one.

### 4.3. Ask/Tell

**Interview**

*Initial setting up:* Two children present. Place on the table in front of the children some pencils, a book, a doll, a box of play foods, crayons, coloring sheets, a tray, figures of Donald Duck and Mickey Mouse, Bozo and Pluto Pup.

*Interview:*
1. *Introduction*
   Tell me your name.
   Tell me your age.
   I'll tell you what you're going to do here. We're going to play some games with the things on the table. (Pick up Donald Duck) For instance, you'll make him do some things. Can you tell me who he is? And you'll play with this doll, too. Later you'll feed her. And you'll color in these shapes.
2. *Test simple constructions, ask$_q$*
   But first, I'd like you to ask X some things, like
   Will you ask X what time it is?
   And will you ask X his last name?
   Ask X his teacher's name.
   Ok, now I want you to *tell* X some things, too, like
   Tell X how many pencils there are here.
   And tell X what color this crayon is.
   Ok, now tell X who this is. (Indicate Bozo)
   And would you ask X what's in this box.
   (Pour food onto tray)
3. *Test complex constructions, ask$_q$*
   Now we're going to feed the doll. You did that very nicely, keeping straight whether you're supposed to ask or tell. Now I want you

to do some more asking and telling, connected with feeding the doll. She's hungry, and you're going to give her this food. Sometimes X will feed her, too. Listen and I'll tell you how.

Would you first ask X what to feed the doll.

Now would you tell X what to feed the doll.

And ask X what to give her next.

Ask X what to feed her.

Would you tell X what to give her.

Ask X what you should feed her now.

(Intersperse a few instructions to partner.)

Now one by one, we're going to put the food back in the box.

Will you ask X what to put back first.

And ask X what to put back next.

Tell X what to put back.

Ask X what food to put back next.

Ask X what you should put back now.

(Intersperse some instructions to partner.)

(Place coloring sheets in front of each child, and crayons where both can reach.)

Now you're going to color in these shapes, again with asking and telling each other what colors to use.

Will you first tell X what color to make the square.

And ask X what color to make the circle.

(Proceed until all the shapes are colored in.)

4. *Test ask*$_r$

Ask X to stand up.

Tell X to walk over to the window.

Ask X to come back.

Ask X to go back to class.      (Partner leaves)

(Line up four figures on the table.)

Now here are all the toys standing in line.

Who is first in line?

Suppose Donald Duck asks to go first in line.

What does he say? How does he ask to go first in line?

Ok, yes, he may. Put him there. Now suppose Mickey Mouse asks Bozo to go first. What does Mickey say?

**Discussion**

*Test Construction:* (C) *John asked/told Bill what to do.*

*Nature of complexity:* A conflict exists between two of the potential syntactic structures associated with a particular verb.

In this interview we questioned the children about a variety of structures associated with the words *ask* and *tell*. Our original intention was to test the children's knowledge of the contrast

(50)  I asked him what to do.
(51)  I told him what to do.

to see if they were able to correctly assign different subjects to the complement verb *do* in the two cases. If a child's grammar includes this distinction in subject assignment, he will interpret these two Ss as follows:

(52)  I asked him what to do. →
         I asked him what *I* should do.
(53)  I told him what to do. →
         I told him what *he* should do.

To make this distinction, the child must have learned that the generally applicable Minimal Distance Principle (MDP) discussed in §2(C) does not apply in the exceptional case of (50). In (50) the subject of the complement verb *do* is not the first NP preceding it, *him,* but instead it is the second NP preceding it, *I.* We hypothesized in §2(C) that the child who has not yet learned to violate the MDP in the case of Ss like (50) will assign *him* as subject of the complement verb *do,* and report interpretations such as

(54)  I asked him what he should do.
(55)  I asked him what he was going to do.

or something similar.

We proceeded to test this distinction informally with a number of 5-year-old and 6-year-old children in the neighborhood, having them carry out instructions such as

(56)  Ask Laura what to feed the doll.
(57)  Tell Laura which food to put back in the box.

Two children were seated at a table on which was placed a doll and some play foods. We explained to them that they were going to feed the doll and that we would tell them how to go about it. We gave them a series of instructions containing *ask* and *tell* followed by the test construction *wh-* + *to* + *inf vb* (wh- clause, subject omitted):

Ask Laura what to feed the doll.
Tell Laura what food to give her.
Ask Laura which food to put back in the box.
Ask Laura what piece of food to pick up.

**Figure 4.3.** *Ask/tell* Experiment. Equipment used for instructions: Ask/tell Barbara what to feed the doll. Ask/tell Barbara what food to put in the box.

Almost immediately we discovered that this distinction was much too sophisticated for the children, and that we were asking far too hard a question, especially of the younger children. The exchanges went about as follows:

Ask Joe what to feed the doll.
*The cucumber*
Now tell Joe what to feed the doll.
*The tomato*
Now ask Joe which food to put back in the box.
*The hot dog*
And ask Joe which piece of food to pick up.
*The watermelon*

The answers came readily, with no hesitation, and with great assurance. This happened with such regularity and with so many children that we finally became suspicious, and called some of them back for some more questions. This time we gave them Ss containing *ask* and *tell* followed by two simpler constructions:

*Noun phrase:* his last name, this doll's name
*wh- clause, subject supplied:* what time it is, who this is

To our surprise, these were the responses:

Ask Joe his last name.
*Foster*
Tell Joe this doll's name.
*Chatty Cathy*
Ask Joe what time it is.
*I don't know what time it is*
Ask Joe who this is.
*Bozo*

These 5-year-olds and 6-year-olds, apparently, were interpreting *ask* all the way through as if we had said *tell*. Their answers indicated no awareness of the fact that in some cases they were instructed to ask, and in others to tell. They simply did not notice or even seem to hear the difference. This phenomenon of 'mixing up' *ask* and *tell* will be recognized as familiar by many parents and teachers of young children. Our study later revealed that the children are not, in fact, mixing up the two at this stage, but merely imposing a *tell* interpretation on both words.[7] Under such circumstances it was clear that the distinction

7. Children in other stages of development did in fact give evidence of mixing up the two words. This confusion, we believe, represents a later rather than an earlier stage of development, and will be discussed in detail below.

in complement subject assignment following *ask* and *tell* that we originally set out to test was not being tested at all. We had wanted to find out specifically if a child knows that in wh- infinitive complements, *ask,* as opposed to *tell,* signals violation of the MDP. This is a specialized aspect of his processing of the word *ask.* When we find that in our test situation he is apparently not processing *ask* at all as different from *tell,* we can hardly expect to learn anything about our more specialized question concerning *ask* and the MDP.

The observation that many 5-year-olds and 6-year-olds respond to this test situation by assigning a *tell* interpretation to all instructions is of course interesting, but the question nevertheless remained of how to relate it to our proposed investigation of the MDP and its exceptions. Clearly we would have to go to older children to find a resolution of the more basic *ask/tell* problem and proceed from there. Or we could shift the emphasis of the investigation on the basis of these preliminary findings, and proceed to explore the *ask/tell* distinction more .generally, considering the MDP question in the context of *ask/tell* processing in general. We chose to follow this latter course, and the results of the more detailed study of *ask* and *tell* have justified the decision. What we found was a fairly well-defined pattern of stages of development with respect to *ask* and *tell,* in which success with our original test question (violation of MDP) constitutes the most advanced stage. A full description follows.

Four constructions associated with *ask* and *tell* were selected for investigation. The first checked the child's interpretation of $ask_r$ in the sense of *request* (German *bitten*), and the next three checked his interpretation of $ask_q$ in the sense of *question* (German *fragen*). The constructions and sample sentence types are presented in Table 4.3.

The $ask_r$ construction is the simplest for our test situation, as the same response is acceptable for both $ask_r$ and *tell.* Subject assignment for complement verb is the same following both $ask_r$ and *tell,* and a single response to both suffices.[8] The $ask_q$ constructions, on the other hand, all require a different response for $ask_q$ and *tell.* In response to $ask_q$, a question must be formulated. Case 1 (wh- clause, subject

8. We did not pursue the distinction between the Rs:
Ask L to leave the room.    →
    *Will you please leave the room.*
Tell L to leave the room.    →
    *Leave the room.*
but accepted either as correct. The child who discriminates between *ask* and *tell* may or may not indicate this distinction in his response, since the differentiation is not obligatory. It would be useful to investigate children's awareness of this distinction, as it might reveal an additional stage of *ask/tell* differentiation, perhaps earlier than the sequence observed here.

**Table 4.3.** Constructions Used in *ask/tell* Interview, Listed in Order of Increasing Complexity. (a) ask$_r$ = *ask* used in request sense (German *bitten*); (b–d) ask$_q$ = *ask* used in question sense (German *fragen*).

---

*ask*$_r$ constructions:     ask/tell + (obj) + to + inf vb
a.   Bozo asks to go first in line. (no *tell* equivalent)
     Bozo asks/tells Mickey to go first in line.

---

*ask*$_q$ constructions
b.   Case 1.          wh- clause, subject supplied
     Ask/tell Laura what color this is.
     Ask/tell Laura what you/she should feed the doll.
     Ask/tell Laura how many pencils there are here.
     Ask/tell Laura who this is.

c.   Case 2.          noun phrase
     Ask/tell Laura her/your last name.
     Ask/tell Laura the color of this book.
     Ask/tell Laura her/your teacher's name.

d.   Case 3.          wh- clause, subject omitted
     Ask/tell Laura what to feed the doll.
     Ask/tell Laura which food to put in the box.
     Ask/tell Laura what to put back next.
     Ask/tell Laura what color to make the square.

---

supplied) is the simplest of these in that there have been no deletions from the complement clause that must be filled in to form the question.

what color is this   →   What color is that?
(complement clause)     (resulting question)

In case 2 (noun phrase), the complement clause is abbreviated, and the question word and verb must be supplied by the listener.

her last name     →     What's your last name?
(complement clause)     (resulting question)

Case 3 (wh- clause, subject omitted) is also abbreviated: subject and auxiliary verb must be supplied.

what to feed the doll   →   What should I feed the doll?
(complement clause)     (resulting question)

We consider that filling in the deletion is more difficult in case 3 than in case 2 since in case 3 the listener must refer outside of the complement clause to retrieve the subject, and choose between two possibilities: NP$_1$ or NP$_2$. In case 2 the listener need not refer outside of the complement clause or make a choice, since the deletions involve only the complement clause itself.

A variety of Ss of these four constructions were presented to the children for their interpretation. An example of the interview form from which we worked is given at the beginning of this section. This interview sample is indicative of the general line of questioning which we pursued with the children, but we did not stick to it rigidly. The interview was carried out in a fairly casual manner, with a good bit of variation depending on the reactions of the child. We varied the explanatory portions according not only to the age of the child, but also to the ease with which he seemed to understand the explanations. We also took pains to vary the order of instructions within a section, in order to avoid insofar as possible the effects of carryover from one instruction to the next, and to avoid establishing a mental set favoring *ask* or *tell*. Sometimes we opened the instruction series with *ask,* and sometimes with *tell*. We also varied the number of instructions in each section according to a child's successes and failures. If a child was failing with a particular construction, it was naturally more interesting and we inserted some additional Ss of this construction to provide greater validity. If a child showed a notable lack of consistency in his responses (and for some children inconsistency seemed to be the order of the day) we would also repeat those particular constructions, with some variation in wording to avoid repetitiveness. In general the interview concentrated on the area of difficulty for each individual child, and we attempted to explore as fully as possible the constructions with which he had the most trouble.

The particular interview techniques that we eventually used, we think, do indicate the children's interpretations quite reliably. We will describe them in some detail, because clearly a great deal of what we claim to 'find out' depends on the way in which we ask the questions.

The best experimental procedure turned out to be to have present during most of the interview two children who knew each other well, only one of whom was being tested. The second child provided a conversation partner for the interviewee, and helped to reduce the artificiality of the interviewing situation. The two children were seated at a table on which a variety of objects were placed, such as a doll, play foods, a box, pencils, books, crayons, coloring sheets, figures of Mickey Mouse and Bozo the Clown, and the like. We explained to the child that he was going to do things like feed the doll, put the food away, color in some sheets, and so on, and that he would do some of these things together with his partner and some by himself. Then followed this sequence.

> But first, I want you to ask P some things, like
>  Ask P what time it is.
>  Ask P his last name.
>  Ask P his teacher's name.
> Ok. Now I want you to *tell* P some things, too, like
>  Tell P how many pencils there are here.
>  And tell P what color this crayon is.
> Ok. Now ask P who this is. (Indicate Bozo)
>  And tell P what color this book is.
>  Would you ask P what's in this box.

## First Interview Sequence for Ask$_q$/Tell

> Includes case 1 Ss: wh- clause, subject supplied
> Includes case 2 Ss: noun phrase

The purpose of these Ss was to determine if the child responded differently to *ask* and *tell* in the simple constructions, cases 1 and 2. The order was varied so that with some children we began with a *tell* instruction, and with others, an *ask* instruction. The actual sequences of *ask* and *tell* were varied to avoid alternation on the one hand, and too long a sequence of *asks* and *tells* on the other. In general we gave the children as much help as possible in overcoming the tendency to simply repeat a response from a preceding instruction without really attending to the command portion of the new instruction. We often requested the child to check his own responses by saying

> "Did you ask him or tell him that time?"

or prefaced an instruction with a cautionary phrase:

> "Now listen carefully, because I don't want you to *tell* P anything this time. I want you to *ask* him who this is."

Throughout the interview our attempt was not to question the child according to a strictly predetermined procedure, but rather to work with him in an exploratory fashion, adjusting the conversation and questions to his responses, asking him to pay attention to his inconsistencies, and asking him frequently to consider and discuss his responses. The children were surprisingly cooperative and willing informants. We felt that during the interviews they were really 'trying their best' to do what was being asked of them, and that their answers were in a very real sense indicative of their knowledge and abilities. They seemed to enjoy being asked to introspect and think, and they had a good time playing along at the game.

The second interview sequence introduced case 3, the complex construction with subject missing. The final instruction of the preceding sequence was always

Ask P what's in this box.

The answer was *food,* and we poured the food onto the tray. Then the interview proceeded as follows.

---

Now we're going to feed the doll. You did very nicely up till now, keeping straight whether you're supposed to ask or tell. Now I want you to do some more asking and telling, connected with feeding the doll. She's hungry, and you're going to give her this food. Sometimes P will feed her, too. Listen and I'll tell you how to go about it.

(For those children who had not kept *ask* and *tell* straight during the first part of the interview, I omitted the reference to correct differentiation.)

Would you first ask P what to feed the doll.

Now would you tell P what to feed the doll.

And ask P what to give her.

Ask P what to feed her next.

Would you tell P what to give her.

Ask P what you should feed her now.

Now one by one, we're going to put the food back in the box.

Will you ask P what to put back first.

And ask P what to put back next.

Tell P what to put back.

Ask P what food to put back now.

Ask P what you should put back now.

(Place coloring sheets in front of each child and crayons where both can reach.)

Now you're going to color in these shapes, again with asking and telling each other what colors to use.

Will you first tell P what color to make the square.

And ask P what color to make the circle.

.
.
.

(Proceed until all shapes are colored in.)

---

**Second Interview Sequence for Ask$_q$/Tell**

Includes case 3 Ss: wh- clause, subject omitted

Includes a few case 1 Ss, interspersed

The purpose of these Ss was to determine if the child responded differently to *ask* and *tell* in our complex construction, case 3, and if so, if he was in addition able to assign the correct subject to the complement verb. Again in this portion of the interview we adjusted the questioning to the individual child, and allowed his responses to determine the succeeding instructions.

The third and final interview sequence checked the children's interpretations of *ask* used in the sense of *request* ($ask_r$). Here the children were given instructions to carry out, as in the first two sequences, and also nonimperative Ss to interpret.

---

Ask P to stand up.
Tell P to walk over to the window.
Ask P to come back.
Ask P to go back to class.
(Partner leaves. Line up four figures on the table.)
Now here are all the toys standing in line.
Who is first in line?
Suppose Donald Duck asks to go first in line.
What does he say? How does he ask to go first in line?
Ok, put him there. Now suppose Mickey Mouse asks Bozo to go first.
What does he say?
Ok, put him there.

---

**Third Interview Sequence for Ask$_r$/Tell**
Includes the construction:
ask/tell + (obj) + to + inf vb

This is the simplest task, for no distinction is required between the responses to the *ask* instructions and the *tell* instructions. The only differentiated response which does indicate two wholly different S analyses is in the S

Mickey Mouse asks Bozo to go first in line.

for which the subject of the complement verb *go* may, in the S's less likely interpretation, be *Mickey Mouse*.

The results that we obtained revealed a good deal of variety in the children's interpretations of the $ask_q$ constructions, ranging from success throughout, through partial errors, all the way to almost total failure. By success we mean that the child's responses (Rs) to the *ask* and *tell* instructions are correctly differentiated. By failure we mean that his Rs are in one way or another not correctly differentiated. Although there was only one way to be right, there were, we found, many different ways to be wrong. These different kinds of failure, or lack of accurate differentiation, seem to reflect varying degrees of knowledge and will be described and illustrated fully below.

The results indicate that the children's knowledge can be characterized in five distinct stages of development. These stages reflect their varying interpretations of $ask_q$ cases 1, 2, and 3. The constructions with $ask_r$ posed no problem and were interpreted correctly by all the children. We will illustrate the Rs to the $ask_r$ construction first, and then proceed to the $ask_q$ construction.

Under the $ask_r$ construction, we checked the children's interpretations of

> Ask P to stand up.
> Tell P to sit down.
> How does Mickey ask to go first in line?
> How does Donald ask Bozo to go first in line?

We pointed out earlier that in these Ss the same R is acceptable for both *ask* and *tell*. The first NP preceding the complement verb is its subject in all these Ss. The children indicated their knowledge of this similarity in subject assignment in their Rs. In our interview transcriptions, the subject's Rs are italicized and indented. The remarks of the child serving as the subject's partner are parenthesized and placed to the right.

> *Eric H., 5.2* (5 years, 2 months)
> Here are all the toys standing in line. Who is first in line?
> > *Mickey Mouse*
> Suppose Donald Duck asks to go first. What does he say?
> > *Can I go first?*
> Ok, yes. Put him there. Now suppose Mickey Mouse asks Bozo to go first. What does Mickey say?
> > *Bozo, go first*

> *Peter B., 5.2*
> Tell X to stand up.
> > *Stand up*
> Ask X to walk across the room.
> > *Walk across the room*

(Line up toys.) Suppose Bozo asks to go first. What does he say?
*Please*
Suppose Mickey asks Donald to go first. What does he say?
*You wanna go in line first?*

*Kim M., 9.7*
Kim, if you're in class and you ask to leave the room, what do you say to the teacher?
*May I please go to the bathroom?*
And suppose you ask Donald to leave the room, what would you say to Donald?
*Would you leave the room, please*

Only one child of the forty assigned the less likely interpretation to the ambiguous S

A asks B to leave the room.

assigning A as complement subject in violation of the MDP. This child was one of the most advanced in our sample, giving evidence of complete control of the MDP and its exceptions, and getting everything right in all of our interviews. He responded as follows.

*Warren H., 9.7*
Warren, suppose you're in class and you ask to leave the room. What would you say to the teacher?
*May I go down to the basement?*
Now suppose you ask Kim to leave the room. What would you say to Kim?
*'Bye*
If you ask Kim to leave the room, who's going to go out? What do you say to her?
*May I go out of the room?*
And suppose you tell Kim to leave the room. What do you say?
*Kim, would you please leave the room*

We will now take up the children's Rs to the *ask*$_q$ constructions of cases 1, 2, and 3. We have said that the children's knowledge can be analyzed into five stages of development. By this we mean that when we characterize the interpretations of each child, we find that our data groups itself fairly naturally into five categories. Furthermore, a definite hierarchy is discernible among these categories. It is possible to line them up, so to speak, so that they constitute an orderly sequence. All of the children learned to handle the simple cases before the complex ones. A child who failed at cases 1 and 2 also failed at case 3, and a child who succeeded at 3 always succeeded at 1 and 2 as well. A child who failed case 3 might succeed at 1 and 2, but never the reverse. This latter point is the important one in terms of developmental stages. The result of it is that our sequence of categories based on data from different children looks very much like a picture of gradual development that a single child might pass through. We would venture that it is likely that an individual child passes through these stages in the order given here (although he perhaps may skip some of them) during his years of actively on-going language acquisition. These five stages are presented in Table 4.4.

**Table 4.4.** Stages of Development in *ask/tell* Differentiation in Children Ages 5 to 10. Success: *ask* response to *ask* instructions; *tell* response to *tell* instructions. Failure: similar responses to *ask* and *tell* instructions. Case 1: Ask/tell Laura what time it is (wh- clause, subject supplied). Case 2: Ask/tell Laura her/your last name (NP). Case 3: Ask/tell Laura what to feed the doll (wh- clause, subject omitted).

|  | *Success* | *Failure* |
| --- | --- | --- |
| Stage A | — | Cases 1, 2, 3 |
| Stage B | Case 1 | Cases 2, 3 |
| Stage C | Cases 1, 2 | Case 3 |
| Stage D | Cases 1, 2, (3)* | (Case 3)* |
| Stage E | Cases 1, 2, 3 | — |

* Parentheses indicate partial success with case 3: *ask* response to *ask* instruction, but wrong subject assigned to complement verb.

We will present a brief description of each of these five stages, with characteristic examples drawn from the interviews. A more detailed analysis, with more complete interviews presented and discussed, follows this general survey.

### 4.3.1. Stage A. Failure: All Cases
8 children: boys: 5.0, 5.1, 5.2, 5.3', 7.6; girls: 5.1', 5.3, 7.1

Children in stage A process *ask* and *tell* alike for all constructions, imposing a *tell* interpretation everywhere. We found this to be the rule rather than the exception for the 5-year-olds. A typical example is Christine M., 5.1.

*Christine M., 5.1*
Ask Eric his last name.
  *Handel*
Ask Eric this doll's name.
  *I don't know*
Ask Eric what time it is.
  *I don't know, how to tell time*
Tell Eric what class is in the library.
  *Kindergarten*
Ask Eric who his teacher is.
  *Miss Turner*
Ask Eric who this is.
  *Bozo*

## 4.3.2. Stage B. Success: Case 1; Failure: Cases 2, 3
2 children: boy: 6.9; girl: 6.6

We found two children who distinguish *ask* and *tell* for case 1, but not for cases 2 or 3. That is, they handle our two simple cases of *wh- clause, subject supplied* and NP differently, succeeding with the former and failing with the latter. They also fail for case 3. (We did not find any children who fail at case 1 and succeed at cases 2 or 3.)

*Peter F., 6.9*
Ask Joanna the color of Mickey Mouse's trousers.
  *Blue*
Tell Joanna who this is.
  *Bozo*
Ask Joanna who this is.
  *Who's that?*          (Pluto)
Tell Joanna what color this book is.
  *Blue*

*Laurie M., 6.6*
Ask Peter the color of the doll's dress.
  *Red*
Ask Peter what color this tray is.
  *What color's it?*

## 4.3.3. Stage C. Success: Cases 1, 2; Failure: Case 3
9 children: boys: 5.2′, 5.3″, 7.9, 8.5, 9.2; girls: 6.5, 6.5′, 9.7, 10.0

Beyond age 6 we begin to find children who succeed in cases 1 and 2, but who still fail to distinguish *ask* and *tell* for case 3. This is a fairly common stage, and the children in it produce sequences like the following.

> *Laura S., 6.5*
> Ask Joanne what color this book is.
> > *What color's that book?*
> Ask Joanne her last name.
> > *What's your last name?*
> Tell Joanne what color this tray is.
> > *Tan*
> Ask Joanne what's in the box.
> > *What's in the box?*
> Ask Joanne what to feed the doll.
> > *The hot dog*
> Now I want you to *ask* Joanne something. *Ask* her what to feed the doll.
> > *The piece of bread*
> Ask Joanne what *you* should feed the doll. (Case 1)
> > *What should I feed the doll?*

With this stage, the results were becoming more interesting, because the children were getting cases 1 and 2 correct, but failing at case 3. Clearly they knew the correct interpretation of *ask* in simple constructions, but could not process it correctly in the more complicated constructions of case 3. Ability to interpret it in simple constructions was somehow not enough. They still interpret it as *tell* in complex constructions.

We concluded that the stage C interpretations were *tell* interpretations for *ask* rather than overapplication of the MDP, because of the fact that the children are telling, and not asking. It is not just that they assign the wrong subject. They also fail to *ask* anything. It is interesting to observe what happens with these children when they are "pressured" to give an *ask* response. It turns out that they cannot seem to formulate a question in response to the instruction

> Ask M what to feed the doll.

even when their attention is drawn to the word *ask* and they are specifically instructed to ask a question. The following exchange illustrates this nicely. This exchange for Laura S. immediately followed the one presented above.

*Laura S., 6.5*
Now listen carefully, because I want you to ask a question. I don't want you to tell her this time. I want you to *ask* Joanne what to feed the doll.
*Feed the doll something*
Ask Joanne what to put back in the box.
*Put back something*

The best she could do was to supply an indefinite instead of an interrogative.

The next child was also unable to supply an interrogative when 'prodded.' He just didn't get it, as he explained.

*Samuel B., 8.5*
Ask Ellen what to feed the doll.
*Feed her hamburgers*
All right now, tell Ellen what to feed her.
*Again?*
M-hm.
*Tomato*
Now I want you to *ask* Ellen something. I want you to *ask* her what to feed the doll.
*Feed her this thing, whatever it's called*
All right. Now listen very carefully, because I don't want you to *tell* her anything this time. I want you to ask her a question. I want you to *ask* her what to feed the doll. Can you do that?
*Let's see. I don't get it*
Ok, just go ahead and ask her what to feed the doll.
*Feed her eggs*

### 4.3.4. Stage D. Success: Cases 1, 2, (3); Wrong Subject: Case 3
6 children: boys: 6.10, 8.4, 8.8; girls: 6.9', 7.0, 8.7

In stage D the children succeed in distinguishing *ask* and *tell* for all three cases, but they get case 3 only half right. That is, for case 3 they ask a question, but they assign the wrong subject to the complement verb. This stage of development lends support to the view that in stage C the children are processing *ask* and *tell* alike for case 3. In stage D we see that the children are in fact distinguishing *ask* and *tell,* as evidenced by the fact that they ask a question in response to the instructions containing *ask.* But at the same time they assign the wrong subject. They assign a subject in accordance with the MDP, which gives the partner, instead of the child to whom the instruction is addressed. To the instruction

Ask Lynn what to put back in the box.

they answer

*What are you going to put in the box?*

This is the stage we had originally set out to find; namely, one in which *ask* and *tell* are distinguished, but in which the exception to the MDP has not yet been learned. There were several different types of responses in this stage, as illustrated by the following exchanges.

> *Joanna B., 6.9*
> Ask Peter what to feed Pluto.
>> *What should you feed Pluto?*

> *Steven B., 8.8*
> Ask Lynn what to feed the dog.
>> *What do you wanna feed the dog?*
> Ask Lynn what to feed the dog.
>> *What do you feed the dog?*
> Ask Lynn what to put in the box.
>> *What are you going to put in the box?*

> *Steven V., 8.4*
> Ask Bryan what food to put back in the box.
>> *What kind of food do you want to put back?*
> Ask Bryan what to put back.
>> *Bryan, what do you want to put back in the box?*

The children came up with still other responses in this stage. They all had in common that they could not supply the correct subject, but their manner of coping with the situation varied. A number of children seemed to bypass the problem of assigning a specific subject by resorting to an impersonal usage similar to French *on.*

> *Penny O., 7.0*
> Ask Ann what to feed the doll.
>> *What d'you feed the doll?*
> Ask Ann what to feed the doll.
>> *What d'ya feed the doll?*
> Ask Ann what to put back in the box.
>> *What d'ya put back?*

*Ann M., 8.7*
Ask Barbara what to feed the doll.
   *What are you supposed to feed the doll?*
Ask Barbara what to feed the doll.
   *Whadda ya feed the doll?*
Ask Barbara what food to put back.
   *What food do you put back?*

And others seemed quite at a loss even to answer grammatically. They merely repeated the *wh- clause* word for word, indicating that they were not really processing the construction at all. We put the child below at stage D because he does in fact distinguish *ask* and *tell*, in that he responds with the *wh- clause* repetition only to *ask,* and responds correctly to *tell*. In a curious fashion, he fails to achieve any grammatical analysis of the *ask* construction. It is as if his rule system makes a try, and reports "Can't handle it." He is left with no analysis.

*Jimmy H., 6.10*
Ask Lee what to feed the doll.
   *What to feed the doll*
Ask Lee what to feed the doll.
   *What to feed the doll*
Tell Lee what to put into the box.
   *Put a tomato into the box*
Ask Lee what to put into the box
   *What to put into the box*

**4.3.5. Stage E. Success: All Cases; Correct Subject: Case 3**
14 children: boys: 5.10, 6.7, 7.3, 8.2, 9.7′, 9.7″, 9.8, 9.9; girls: 7.0′, 7.2, 8.6, 8.8′, 9.1, 9.8′

Children in stage E succeed with all three cases. They produce exchanges like the following with no trouble or hesitation.

*Warren H., 9.7*
Ask Kim what to feed the doll.
   *What should I feed the doll?*
Ask Kim what to put back in the box.
   *What should I put back in the box?*
Tell Kim what color to make the circle.
   *Make the circle red*
And ask Kim what color to make the square.
   *What color should I make the square?*

This was the final stage. In this stage, the processing of all the test constructions was carried out in accordance with the rules of adult grammar.

We can now turn to the more detailed discussion of these stages. We would like to preface this discussion with a few remarks. The first point that we would like to make concerns the ages at which the children were observed to be in the various stages. The children did not give evidence of these stages with a regular progression by age. We had one child of 5.10 who succeeded for all constructions, right down to and including stage E. And we had a 10-year-old who turned out to be at stage C, with *ask* and *tell* still processed alike for case 3. These are the extremes, but in general there was a good bit of variation. It was interesting to note also that in a given age group, the relative development of the children did not in all cases coincide with the teacher's assessment of their classroom performance. That is, it was not the 'brighter' children (so classified by their teacher) who necessarily proved to be at a later stage of this particular linguistic development. In grade 2 the boy who was at the most advanced stage of development (stage E, in fact — the only second-grade boy in our sample to reach this stage) was a child whose classroom performance was rated by his teacher as below average. The significant thing is that all of these stages exist, and can be observed and ascertained with reliability. If we characterize the interpretations of each child as fully as possible, and then line them up by degree of knowledge rather than by age, what emerges is an orderly sequence. We cannot specify *when* a child will reach a particular stage of development, but we can draw a conclusion about the order in which he will go through them.

The second point concerns what appear to be periods of transition from stage to stage. Not all the children interviewed gave evidence of being neatly in one stage or another. There were several instructions given to the children for each construction, and sometimes they answered inconsistently. We interpreted these inconsistencies as an indication that the child was in a state of transition from one stage to the next. This happened primarily between stages A and B. The following exchange is a case in point.

> *Scotty G., 5.0*
> Ask Christine her last name.
>> *I don't know*
> Ask Christine what the doll's name is.
>> *What is her name?*

Tell Christine what color this book is.
> *Blue*

Ask Christine what time it is.
> *I don't know*

Tell Christine how old she is.
> *How old are you?*

Tell her what color the doll's dress is.
> *What color's the doll's dress?*

This child is getting both his *tells* and his *asks* wrong. Although on the surface he seems to be doing *worse* than the stage A children, who consistently get *tell* right, we interpret his responses to mean that he has abandoned stage A (all *tell*) and begun to introduce *ask*, albeit imperfectly as yet. He is in a state of transition between interpreting everything as *tell*, and correctly differentiating *ask* and *tell*. This will be discussed more fully under stage A below.

Our last point is a statement of caution regarding our intentions in presenting the detailed analysis which follows. We interviewed a relatively small number of children, eight from each grade, forty in all. Given this small number, it is quite possible that the details of our findings may not be borne out by a more extensive study. Accordingly, in what follows, much of what we say must be understood as tentative and primarily suggestive. The interest of our results lies in the overall picture of stages of development leading from simple grammatical tasks to more complex ones. The overall picture is a clear one and the validity of this material rests more in its general guidelines than in its specific details.

We will now proceed to the detailed discussion, and a presentation of sample interviews.

### 4.3.6. Stage A. Failure: All Cases
8 children: boys: 5.0, 5.1, 5.2, 5.3', 7.6; girls: 5.1', 5.3, 7.1

Children in stage A are characterized by poor *ask/tell* differentiation for all cases, simple as well as complex. They respond alike to *ask* instructions and *tell* instructions, and do a poor job of correcting their errors when requested to reflect on and reconsider their responses. Some of these children are quite consistent in favoring the *tell* response, irrespective of the instruction, and these are presented below as Group A. The others are by contrast inconsistent, in that they give both *ask* and *tell* responses freely, but not necessarily to appropriate instructions. These children are presented below as Group A+.

*Group A*
4 children: boys: 5.1, 5.2; girls: 5.1', 5.3

These children display a strong tendency to respond to both *ask* and *tell* instructions by telling, and the *ask* response in our interviews is either absent or very marginal. They give *tell* Rs to many *ask* instructions, but never give *ask* Rs to *tell* instructions. One example is Christine M., 5.1', who gave all *tell* responses.

> *Christine M., 5.1'*
> I want you to ask Eric some things. Will you ask Eric his last
>     name.
>> *Handel*
> Ask Eric the doll's name.
>> *I don't know*
> That's right. You don't. Ask Eric what time it is.
>> *I don't know, how to tell time*
> Tell Eric what class is in the library.
>> *Kindergarten*
> Ask Eric who his teacher is.
>> *Miss Turner*

Suppose you ask your friend to come over and play. What would you say? You want to ask your friend to come over and play this afternoon.
1 →    *Could you come over and play this afternoon?*
Ask Eric to come over and play this afternoon.
>> *Come over and play this afternoon*                    (No.)
Ask Eric who this is.
2 →    *Bozo*

Notice that this child, Christine M., formulates a request in response to $ask_r$ (1 → ), and returns to telling in response to $ask_q$ (2 → ).

A second example illustrating predominant *tell* responses is Barbara M., 5.3. This child persists with *tell* Rs even in the case of the final instruction (2 → )

> Ask L what *you* should feed her.

which she herself recognizes as unlikely.

*Barbara M., 5.3*
First I'd like you to ask Linda some things. Think you can ask Linda some questions? Ask Linda what time it is.
>*I don't know*

Ask Linda her last name.
>*La Croix*

Ask Linda her teacher's name.
>*Miss Turner*

Now I want you to tell Linda some more things. Tell Linda how many pencils there are here.
>*Three*

And tell Linda what color this crayon is.
>*Yellow*

And ask Linda what's in this box.
>*I don't know*

Could you ask Linda? Maybe Linda knows.

1 →    *Do you, Linda?*                    (No.)
I'll show you what's in the box.
>*A doll!*

She's hungry. Barbara, will you ask Linda what to feed her first.
>*This*

What is it?
>*Watermelon*

Linda, tell Barbara what to feed her next.      (Eggs)

2 →    Barbara, ask Linda what *you* should feed her.
>*Ask Linda what* I *should feed her?*
>          (addressed to interviewer)

M-hm.
>*This*

The one response question that this child did formulate (1 → ) was considerably prompted by context, and was not in response to the given instruction

>Ask Linda what's in the box.

Rather it was an attempt to find out if Linda knew.

A third example is Chris L., for whom the *tell* R predominates. He was able, when pressured, to give one *ask* R each time (arrows) but on subsequent instructions returned to *tell* Rs. It is also interesting that he is apparently unable to say what he has done after asking a question (boxed section).

*Chris L., 5.1*

First, I want you to tell me some things, like, tell me how many pencils there are here.

    *Three*

And I want you to ask Christine some things. Can you *ask* her her last name.

    *Christine McDonough*

Will you ask Christine who this is.

    *Donald Duck*        (I know that)

If you ask your teacher if you can go out of the room so you can go to the bathroom, what do you say to your teacher?

    *Can I go to the bathroom?*

Now if you *ask* Christine what time it is now.

→    *What time is it?*      (I don't know)

It's ten o'clock. Ask Christine what's in this box.

    *I don't know*

Ask her. Maybe she knows.

    *Do you know?*      (No)

Ask Christine what color this book is.

    *Blue*

And will you ask me my name.

    *I don't know*

    (Christine interjects: What's your name?)

It's Mrs. Chomsky. Christine just asked me what my name is. Could *you* ask me now?

    *Mrs. Chomsky*

I think you *told* me what my name is. Will you tell me my name.

    *Mrs. Chomsky*

M-hm. *Ask* Christine what her last name is.

→    *What's your last name?*    (McDonough)

---

What did you just do? Did you ask her something?

    (Silence)

You did!

    *What did I ask her?*

You tell me. What did you ask her?

    *I don't know*

---

Let's do it again. Ask Christine her last name.

    *Christine McDonough*

You *ask* Christine. Can you do that? You have to ask her a question. I want you to ask her what her last name is.

→    *What's your last name?*    (McDonough)

Suppose you ask me what day today is.
    *I don't know.*
Could you ask me? Maybe I know.
    *Thursday*

Ask Christine what color to make the square.
    *Red*

The fourth example is Eric H., 5.2. Again, the *tell* R predominates, and like the preceding child, he is able to give one *ask* R each time when pressured, at least in the simple cases (1 → ), and then returns to *tell* Rs (2 → ). Notice that this child is able to indicate when he has answered by telling (boxed sections).

*Eric H., 5.2*
Ask Peter what color this crayon is.
    *Yellow*
Ask him how many pencils there are here.
    *Three*
Tell him who this is.
    *Mickey Mouse*
Ask him what color this book is.
    *Blue*
Ask him what's in this box.
    *I don't know*
Ask *him*. He knows.
1 →    *What's in the box?*         (A doll)
Ask him what's in the suitcase.
1 →    *What's in the suitcase?*    (A doll and some other stuff)
Ask him who this is.
2 →    *Donald Duck*

> Did you ask him or tell him?
>     *I told him*

Now ask him. Even though you know, ask him who it is.
1 →    *Who is he?*     (Donald Duck)
Ask him who this is.
2 →    *Bozo*

> Did you ask him or tell him?
>     *I told him*

Now ask him.

1 → *Who is that?*      (Bozo)
Ask him the color of this book.
2 → *Blue*

> Did you ask him or tell him?
>   *Tell him*

Now ask him the color of this book.
1 → *What color's the book?*      (Blue)
Ask him the name of this doll.
2 → *Kiddle*

Eric, ask Peter what to feed the dog.
  *Feed the dog the hamburger*
*Ask* Peter what to feed the dog.
      (Peter, prompting: Ask!)
  *A sandwich*
I think you *told* him. Did you ask him anything? Can you figure
out how to *ask* him.
3 → *Feed him a sandwich*
All right.

Now, one by one, we're going to put the food back in the box.
Eric, ask Peter what to put back.
  *Put back the watermelon*

Eric, ask Peter what color to make the square.
  *Make the square orange*
Ask Peter what color you should make the square.      (Case 1)
4 → *What color shall I make the square?*      (Blue)

Notice also that the ability of this child (Eric H.) to correct his R
from telling to asking is limited to the simple cases. In the complex
case he consistently tells, even when pressured (3 →). In contrast,
notice the *ask* R to the final instruction (4 →) which is the simple
construction, case 1, subject supplied.

*Group A* + 4 children: boys: 5.0, 5.3′, 7.6; girls: 7.1

These children also evidence poor *ask/tell* differentiation for all
our constructions, and are inconsistent in their Rs. They display both
*ask* and *tell* Rs. Their trouble is that their Rs are not appropriate to
the instructions. They ask when instructed to tell, and tell when instructed to ask. They also respond appropriately part of the time.

They are considerably influenced by their first response of the series, and tend to repeat this R with subsequent instructions.

The first example is Scotty G., 5.0. He was questioned at two different sessions, several days apart. His Rs are considerably mixed. On day 1, (1 →) indicates his correct Rs, and (2 →) indicates his incorrect Rs. On day 2 he limits himself almost exclusively to asking (3 →). Notice that he is under the impression that he has been telling (4 →). Notice also near the end that he distinguishes case 1 from case 3. For case 1 he asks (5 →), and for case 3 he tells (6 →).

*Scotty G., 5.0          day 1*
First, I want you to tell me some things. Will you tell me how many pencils there are here.
1 → *Three*
And I want you to ask Christine some things, too. Would you ask Christine her last name.
2 → *I don't know her last name*
Well, then, you can't tell her her last name. But do you think you could ask her what it is.
1 → *What's your last name?*      (McDonough)
Would you ask Christine the doll's name.
2 → *I don't know*
Ask Christine what the doll's name is.
1 → *What is her name?*      (I don't know)
Will you ask Christine what time it is.
2 → *I don't know what time it is.*
Ask Christine, then. Ask her the question.
       (Silence)
I'll tell you what. Tell Christine what color this book is.
1 → *Blue*
And ask Christine who her teacher is. Ask her a question. Ask her who her teacher is.
1 → *Who is her teacher?*      (Miss Turner)
Now could you ask her how old she is.
2 → *Five*
Tell Christine how old she is. Go ahead, tell her. Can you hear a difference, Scotty, if I say to you *Tell Christine how old she is.* What do you do if I tell you that?
2 → *How old are you?*      (Five)
What did you tell her?
    *I don't know*

Uh-uh. You don't. It's hard. Ask Donald if he's hungry.

1 → *Are you hungry?*

Tell Bozo your name.

1 → *Scott*

Tell Mickey what's in this box.

1 → *Food*

Ask Pluto what color this book is. *Ask* Pluto what color this book is.

2 → *Blue*


*Scotty G., 5.0          day 2*

I want you to ask Jojo some questions. Will you ask Jojo what time it is.

> *I don't know*
>   (worried sounding)

Ok. If you don't know, just say so. Ask Jojo his last name.

3 → *What's your last name?*      (Jojo Marrazzo)

And ask Jojo his teacher's name.

3 → *What's your teacher's name?*      (Miss Turner)

*Tell* Jojo some things, too. Tell Jojo how many pencils there are here.

3 → *How many pencils are there?*      (Three)

All right, and tell him what color the crayon is.

3 → *What color is the crayon is?*      (Yellow)

And ask him what color the book is.

3 → *What color is the book?*      (Blue)

And ask him who this is.

3 → *What is that? Who is that?*      (Bozo)

And ask him the color of Mickey Mouse's pants.

3 → *What color is Mickey Mouse's pants?*      (Blue)

And tell him what color the doll's dress is.

3 → *What color's the doll's dress?*      (Red, with white spots on it.)

All right, now, could you *tell* him something. Don't ask him this time. Tell him what color the crayon is.

3 → *What color's the crayon is?*      (Yellow)

Did you tell him or ask him?

4 → *I telled him*


Ok. And do you want to color in some shapes? Would you ask Jojo what color to make the circle.

6 → *Color it . . . this color*

(to Jojo): Ok. Joe, tell Scotty what color to make the triangle.
(This color)
And Scotty, would you tell Joe what color he should make the
square.
*Make it this color*
And would you ask Joe what color you should make the circle.
5 → *What color shall I make the circle?* (This color)
Ok. Now will you ask Joe what color you should make the
square.
5 → *What color shall I make the square?*
*Ask* Joe what color to make the triangle. (Triangle still blank)
6 → *This one*

The next three examples illustrate very mixed Rs. The children tend
to continue with a R once they have gotten started. All three are able
to indicate what they did, when questioned, and correct their errors
(arrows), but lose the *ask/tell* distinction again in subsequent Rs.

*Joe M., 5.3*
First I want you to tell me how many pencils there are here.
*Two*
And I want you to ask Peter some things, too, like, will you ask
Peter his last name.
*Peter, what's your last name?* (Bonazoli)
Ask Peter what time it is. Can you ask him what time it is?
*I don't know what time it is*
Can you tell him what color the book is.
*Blue*
Can you ask him what color this crayon is.
*Yellow*
Now listen carefully, because I want you to *ask* him something.
I want you to ask him what this is. Can you do that?
*Peter, what is that?* (Clip)
Now the whole point is to listen whether you're supposed to ask
or tell. Ok? Make sure you've got the difference straight. Ask
Peter what color this is.
*Peter, what color's that?* (Red)
And *tell* Peter what color this is.
*Peter, what color's that?*
Uh-uh. *Tell* him. Can you tell him what color it is?
*Yellow*

Ask Peter what's in the box.
*Peter, what's in the box?*     (Food)
Tell Peter what color the book is.
*Peter, what color's the book is?*     (Blue)
Did you tell him what color the book was, or ask him? Which did you do?

→     *Ask him*

Ok. Can you tell him now, tell him what color the book is.
*Blue*

Ok. Now, if you'll hold on to the doll, you and Peter are going to feed her. And you're going to feed her by asking and telling each other how to do it. Can you, Jojo, tell Peter what to feed her.
*Peter, what to feed her*
I don't think you told him anything. Tell Peter what to feed the doll.
(Silence. Points at toast)
The toast. Peter, will you tell Jojo what to feed her.
(Strawberry)

---

Jojo, ask Peter what to feed her now.
*Feed her the roll*
Put the doll in the box. And *tell* Peter what food to put in the box.
*Peter, put in the strawberry*
Now ask Peter what to put in the box.
*Put in the watermelon*
Ask Peter what *you* should put in the box.
*Peter, what should I put in the box?*     (Hot dog)
Now tell Peter what to put in the box.
*The hot dog*
Jojo, ask Peter what to put in next.
*Peter, put in the roll*
Ask Peter what you should put in next.
*Peter, what could I put in?*     (The piece of toast)

---

*Joe M., 5.3      second session*
Ask Barbara what time it is.
*I don't know*
Ask Barbara her last name.
*What's your last name?*     (Murphy)

Ask Barbara her teacher's name.
> *What's your teacher's name?*    (Miss Turner)

Ask Barbara how many pencils there are here.
> *How many pencils are there?*    (Three)

Tell Barbara what color the pencil is.
> *Not the pencil, the crayon*

Tell her what color the crayon is.
> *Yellow*

And ask her the color of this book.
> *Blue*

Ask her who this is.
> *Donald Duck*

Tell her who this is.
> *Bozo*

Notice for this child, Joe M., that in the boxed section he responds to all the case 3 instructions by telling, and to all the *ask* case 1s by asking.

*Barbara A., 7.1*

Will you ask Kenny how many pencils there are here.
> *Kenny, how many pencils are there?*    (Three)

Will you tell Kenny what color this book is.
> *What color that book is?*    (It's blue)

Will you tell Kenny who this is.
> *Kenny, what's the name of that?*    (Donald Duck)

Did you tell him or ask him who that is?
→ > *I asked him*

Now I said tell. So listen carefully, whether I say tell him or ask him. All right, try and make sure you tell the difference. Ask him who this is.
> *Do I ask him the name or does he tell me?*

Both. You ask him, and then he tells you. Can you ask him who this is?
> *Should I say the name?*

All right.
> (Silence)

Would you find it easier to tell him who it is?
> *Ok* (Silence)

All right, tell him who it is.
> *Um . . . it's Bozo*

All right. And would you ask him who this is.
    *Mickey Mouse*
And would you ask him what color this is.
    *Black*
Did you ask or tell?
→    *Oh*
Can you ask him what color it is.
    *Ok. Kenny, what color is that?*    (Blue)
Good. Now, would you ask him what color this is, this tray.
    *White*
Now will you tell him what's in the suitcase.
    *Kenny, what's in the suitcase?*    (A doll)
And would you tell him what color the book is.
    *Kenny, what color is the book?*    (Blue)
And would you ask him his brother's name.
    *Kenny, what's your brother's name?*    (Steven)
And tell him your brother's name.
    *Should I tell him the name?*
Tell him your brother's name.
    *Steve*
All right, and tell him what color this pencil is.
    *Kenny, what color is that pencil?*    (Yellow)

Would you tell Kenny what to feed the doll first.
    *Kenny, what should I feed the doll?*    (A hot dog)
Ask Kenny what to feed the doll.
    *Kenny, . . .* (To interviewer): *what* he *should feed the doll?*
Tell Kenny what to feed the doll.
    *Kenny, what to feed the doll.*    (A hamburger)
    (Barbara feeds her the hamburger)
And would you ask Kenny what you should feed the doll.
    *Kenny, what should I feed the doll?*    (A watermelon)
Tell Kenny what he should feed the doll.
    *Kenny, what shall you feed the doll?*    (Bread)
And would you ask Kenny what to feed the doll.
    *Kenny, what shall I feed the doll?*    (A pear)
And would you tell Kenny what to feed the doll.
    *Kenny, what shall I feed the doll?*    (The cucumber)

*Kenneth V., 7.6*
I want you to first ask Richard some things. Would you ask
Richard what color this crayon is.

*What color's that crayon?*       (Yellow)

Would you ask Richard the color of this book.

*What's the color of that book?*       (Blue)

And I also want you to *tell* Richard some things. Would you tell Richard how many pencils there are here.

*How much's pencils are there?*       (Three)

And would you tell Richard the color of the doll's dress.

*What's the color of the doll's dress?*       (Red)

And would you tell Richard who this is.

*Who's that?*       (Bozo)

Did you ask him or tell him?

*What?*

Did you ask him or tell him?

→       *I asked him*

Would you tell him this time. Tell him who this is.

*Bozo*

And tell him who this is.

*Donald Duck*

Now listen carefully whether it's tell or ask. All right. Would you tell him the color of this crayon.

*What's the color of the crayon?*       (Yellow)

And would you tell him what color this tray is.

*What's the color  . . .  Oh, it's white*

Yes. And tell him how many pencils.

*How many pencils?*       (Three)

Did you tell or ask?

*Oh, three pencils*

And would you tell him who this is.

*Mickey Mouse*

And would you ask him who this is.

*Who's that?*       (Pluto)


Now, would you two color in these shapes for me.

*All of them?*

One at a time. Now, Kenny, would you ask Richard what color to make the square.

*Green*

(to Richard): Richard, would you tell Kenny what color to make *his* square.

                                        (Yellow)

Kenny, would you ask Richard what color to make the circle.

*Black*

And would you ask Richard what color you should make the triangle.

> *What color should I make the triangle?*      (Blue)

Ask Richard what's in the box.

> *What's in the box?*      (Food)

I'm going to ask you and Richard to feed the doll. Kenny, would you ask Richard which food to give her.

> *Feed her watermelon*

Would you tell Richard what food to give her.

> *A can of milk*

Kenny, ask Richard what you should feed her.

> *Richard, what should I feed her?*      (The tomato)


With respect to the inconsistency evidenced by Group A+, as contrasted with the more consistent behavior of Group A, we would like to propose the hypothesis that the inconsistent A+ child is the more advanced, and is actually in a state of transition from the consistent telling stage to the stage of correct *ask/tell* differentiation. This would mean that the less advanced child seems on the surface to be doing better at certain tasks. For the Group A child who never asks, everything is *tell.* If we look only at his responses to the *tell* instructions, he is scoring perfect. At a later stage the perfect score on *tell* disappears, and his Rs are mixed: some right, some wrong. This is when *ask* is coming in. Still later, he gets all *tell*s right again, and also all *ask*s.

Let us state it a little differently. At the earlier stage, the child appears to be making fewer mistakes. His performance is more orderly. He gets all his *tells* correct, and all his *asks* wrong. At a later stage, his performance becomes disorderly. He begins getting some *ask*s right, but at the same time, also gets some *tell*s wrong! If we look only at his performance with *tell,* he indeed appears to have regressed. Whereas he used to get them all right, now he is getting some wrong, and appears to be really mixed up. He seems to have lost his ability to interpret *tell* correctly.

If we look at it from the point of view of the total system, however, the picture looks different. When he knows no *ask* at all, he has no trouble. Everything is *tell.* As he begins to learn *ask,* what he has to do is take a single set of constructions and divide it into two sets, one *ask* and one *tell.* His initial attempts include errors — it takes a while before he can get straight just how to break this formerly unified set into two new separate ones. He experiments with the *ask* rule, and applies it sometimes too little and sometimes too much. Finally he gets it straight. Thus we conclude that the child who apparently 'knows' *tell* in all its uses is actually at an inferior stage of knowledge compared to the child who is getting *tell* wrong some of the time. For us to appreciate this fact, we need only compare the corresponding performance with *ask* of these two children.

This phenomenon may perhaps be related to the observation reported by Mehler and Bever (1967) in their quantity conservation experiments with young children. They observed that 2.6-year-olds do better than 3.6-year-olds in conserving quantity judgments under various permutations, and hypothesized that the older children may be hampered by overapplying acquired strategies that are as yet unknown to the less experienced younger child. There is a similarity in the notion that the younger child is doing 'better' because he knows less. The transitional period of learning, before the new knowledge has been fully mastered, seems to be characterized by a disruption of the former workable system which results in temporarily increased errors.

### 4.3.7. Stage B. Success: Case 1; Failure: Cases 2, 3
2 children: boy: 6.9; girl: 6.6

The two children whom we have designated as being in stage B distinguish between our two simple cases of *wh- clause* and NP, succeeding with the former and failing with the latter. In response to

Ask L the color of the doll's dress.

they tell, but in response to

Ask L what color this book is.

they ask. They fail also with the complex constructions of case 3.

This stage is the most questionable in our data, since it is based on the Rs of only two children, and we would like to emphasize its tentative status. Our characterization of it as a separate stage is supported by the observation that none of our children distinguish cases 1 and 2 in the reverse manner, i.e., failing at 1 while succeeding at 2. This is in accord with our observation earlier that case 2 is an abbreviated construction that requires the listener to recover deleted items in order to formulate a question, and is thereby more difficult to process than case 1.

Samples from the interviews with these two children are presented below.

> *Laurie M., 6.6*
> Laurie, ask Peter the color of the doll's dress.
>     *Red*
> Ask Peter what color this tray is.
>     *What color's it?*     (White)
> And tell Peter what color your hair is.
>     *Red*
>
> Laurie, ask Peter what to feed Pluto.
>     *Feed Pluto the bean*
> Tell Peter what to feed him now.
>     *An apple*
> Laurie, ask Peter what to put back in the box first.
>     *Put . . . hot dog*
> Tell Peter what to put back.
>     *The apple*

> *Peter F., 6.9*
> Ask Joanna the color of Mickey Mouse's trousers.
>     *Blue*
> Tell Joanna who this is.
>     *Bozo*
> Ask Joanna who this is.
>     *Who's that?*     (Pluto)
> Tell Joanna what color this book is.
>     *Blue*
>
> Peter, ask Joanna what to feed the doll.
>     *Feed her a piece of bread*
> Tell Joanna what to feed the doll.
>     *Feed her a hamburg*
> Ask Joanna what to put back.
>     *The doll*

**4.3.8. Stage C. Success: Cases 1, 2; Failure: Case 3**
9 children: boys: 5.2', 5.3", 7.9, 8.5, 9.2; girls: 6.5, 6.5', 9.7, 10.0

Children in stage C succeed at cases 1 and 2 but fail at case 3. This is a fairly common and very definite stage, in which we find very little inconsistency. The children easily distinguish *ask* and *tell* in the simple cases. They answer quickly, with assurance, and know just what they are doing. They then proceed to fail entirely at case 3, telling straight through. Pressuring them for a change in their incorrect *ask* case 3 Rs is of little avail. Apparently they simply do not and cannot understand this construction other than as *tell*.

A representative child is Peter B., 5.2.

> *Peter B., 5.2*
> I want you to tell me some things, like tell me how many pencils there are here.
>> *Two*
> And I want you to ask Scotty some things, like, ask Scotty his last name.
>> *What's your last name, Scotty?*   (Griggs)
> Ask Scotty what time it is.
>> *What time it is?*
> Tell Scotty what color this book is.
>> *What color this book is, Scotty?*   (Blue)
> Now, could you *tell* him what color it is, instead of asking him.
>> *Blue*
> Tell him who this is.
>> *Donald Duck*
> Now listen. *Ask* him who this is.
>> *Boz — Who's that?*   (Bozo)
> Ask Scotty what's in this box.
>> *Scotty, what's in that box?*   (Food)
> Now Peter, if you'll hold her . . . I want you and Scotty to feed her. But I want you to do it in a special way. So listen carefully, and you're going to tell each other what to give her to eat, and you'll ask each other, too, about feeding her. First, Peter, would you tell Scotty what to feed her.
>> *Feed her the watermelon*
> (To Scotty): All right, Scotty, tell Peter what to feed her.
>> (The strawberry)
> Ok. Peter, *ask* Scotty what to feed her now.
>> *Scotty, feed her the hot dog*
> Now this time, I want you to really ask him something. I want you to *ask* him what to feed her.
> 1 → *Feed her the can of milk*
> Now, Peter, will you put the doll in the box. And will you tell Scotty what food to put in the box with her.
>> *The sandwich*

Now ask Scotty, *ask* Scotty what to put in the box next.
 *The can of milk*
Ask Scotty what *you* should put in the box.    (Case 1)
2 →    *What should I put in the box, Scotty?*    (The strawberry)
Tell Scotty what he should put in the box.
 *Scotty, put in the hot dog*
Ask Scotty what to put in the box.
 *Scotty, put in the watermelon*

Notice that with this child, Peter B., prodding did not help. He stuck to his *tell* R for case 3, even under pressure (1 →). He did give a correct *ask* R subsequently for a case 1 instruction (2 →).

A second child, Paul F., 5.3, is interesting in that prodding changed his R, although it did not result in a correction. It left him at a loss to know what to say (1 →).

*Paul F., 5.3*
I want you to ask Eric some things. Would you ask Eric his last name.
 *What's your last name, Eric?*    (Handel)
Ask him who this is.
 *Who's that?*    (I don't know)
That's Pluto. That's Mickey Mouse's dog. And will you ask Eric what time it is.
 *What time is it, Eric?* (I don't know. I don't know how to tell time)
I do. It's 9:30. And will you tell Eric what color this book is.
 *What color's that book?*
Now wait a minute. I said *tell* him what color the book is.
 *That book is blue, right, you?*
Now you listen whether I'm telling you to tell him or ask him, ok?
Tell him what color the crayon is.
 *Yellow*
Tell him how many pencils there are.
 *Three*
Ask him who this is.
 *Donald . . . no, who's that?*    (Donald Duck)
Tell him who this is.
 *Bozo*
Ask Eric what's in this box.
 *What's in that box, Eric?*    (I don't know)

I'll tell you what's in here. Food. Now Pluto wants to get fed.
And you two are going to do the feeding. But I want you to do
it in a special way. So listen and do it. Paul, will you ask Eric
what to feed the dog.
>  *Eric, feed the dog the watermelon*
Paul —
>  *What?*
I told you to *ask* Eric what to feed the dog. I think you *told* him.
Can you *ask* him this time what to feed the dog.
>  *Eric . . .    (What)*
1 →    (Pause, sigh) *No, what should I say, what should I say?*
Well, how would you ask him what to feed the dog?
>  (Silence)
Can you figure that out?
>  *Ah, no*


The next child, Samuel B., 8.5, responded to prodding in much the
same way. It left him at a loss (1 →). When told to forget it and just
go ahead and ask, he returned to his *tell* R.


> *Samuel B., 8.5*
Will you tell Ellen how many pencils there are here.
>  *Three*
Would you tell Ellen what color this crayon is.
>  *Yellow*
I want you to ask Ellen some things, too, like ask Ellen her last
name.
>  *What's your last name, Ellen?*    (Frank)
Would you ask Ellen what time it is.
>  *What time it is, Ellen?*    (I don't know)
Would you tell Ellen what color that book is.
>  *Blue, with white and black on it*
Would you ask Ellen what's in this box.
>  *What's in the box, Ellen?*    (Food)
All right, now —
>  *That's fruits!*
Some of it. Will you ask Ellen what to feed the doll.
>  *Feed her hamburgers. Hot dog, I mean*
All right, now, tell Ellen what to feed her.
>  *Again?*

M-hm.

*Ah, what's this?*

Tomato.

*A tomato*

Now I want you to *ask* Ellen something. I want you to ask her what to feed the doll.

*Uh, feed her this thing, whatever it's called*

(Ellen): Cucumber

*Oh. Feed her a cucumber*

All right. Now listen very carefully, because I don't want you to *tell* her anything this time. I want you to *ask* her a question. I want you to ask her what to feed the doll. Can you do that?

1 →    *Let's see. I don't get it*

It's impossible, isn't it?

*Yeah*

Ok. All right, just go ahead and ask her what to feed the doll.

*Feed her eggs*

The next child, Elizabeth U., 10.0, varied between straight telling:

*Feed the doll a pear*

and requesting, or asking in the *ask*$_r$ sense:

*Will you feed the doll a tomato*

Notice that she twice observed the correct *ask* R from her partner (arrows) but that she did not react to this modeling.

*Elizabeth U., 10.0*

Would you tell Robin how many pencils there are here.

*Three*

And would you tell Robin what color the tray is.

*White*

And I want you to ask Robin some things, too, like will you ask Robin her last name.

*What's your last name?*       (Matthews)

And will you ask Robin what's in the box.

*What's in the box?*       (Food)

And would you tell Robin what color the book is.

*What color is the book?*

Whoops, *tell* her. Tell her what color the book is.

*Blue*

Ok. And ask her what color the crayon is.

*What color's that crayon?*       (Yellow)

Ok. I want you to be able to keep straight the telling and the asking. So listen very carefully, all right? Now, you're going to feed the doll with telling and asking, and first, Elizabeth, would you ask Robin what to feed the doll.

>    *Feed the doll a pear*

And will you now tell Robin what to feed the doll.

>    *A hot dog*

Now again, would you ask Robin what to feed the doll.

>    *Will you feed the doll a tomato*

Now you'll put the food away into the box. Will you ask Robin what to put away first.

>    *Put the eggs*

(To Robin): Robin, will you ask Elizabeth what to put away.

>                    (The bread)

→ *Ask* her what to put away. (What shall I put away?)

>    *Put the pear*

Now will you ask Robin what to put away.

>    *Put away the hot dog*

(To Robin): And you ask Elizabeth what to put away.

→                    (What should I put away?)

>    *The tomato*

And will you ask Robin what to put away.

>    *Will you put away the bread*

Ask Robin what color to make the square.

>    *Make the square black*

And would you tell Elizabeth what color to make the triangle.

>                    (Yellow)


The next child, Laura S., 6.5, is very interesting. Like the others, she tells in case 3 when instructed to ask. But notice that she responds to prodding. She changes her answer to:

>    *Feed the doll something*

at arrow 1 (1 →). She is unable to supply an interrogative, and compromises with a halfway measure: she supplies the indefinite *something*.


*Laura S., 6.5*

I want you to tell Joanne some things. Will you tell Joanne how many pencils there are here.

>    *Three*

And I want you to ask her some things, too. Would you ask her what color this book is.
*What color's the book?*    (Blue)
All right. And ask Joanne her last name.
*What's your last name?*        (Bonazoli)
And tell Joanne what color this tray is.
*Tan*
Ask Joanne what's in the box.
*What's in the box?*      (Food)
Ok. The doll's hungry, and I'd like you two to feed her, but I want you to do it in a special way, by asking each other how, and telling each other how. Each time you'll either tell Joanne what to feed her, or you'll find out from Joanne what you should feed her, and Joanne will do the same thing. Will you first tell Joanne what to feed her.
*The two eggs*
All right, will you ask Joanne what to feed her now.
*The hot dog*
All right. Now, I want you to ask Joanne something. I want you to ask her what to feed the doll.
*The piece of bread*
Now listen carefully, because I want you to ask a question. I don't want you to tell her this time. I want you to ask Joanne what to feed the doll.

1 →    *Feed the doll something*
You're letting her decide? Ok, good. All right. Now will you ask Joanne what you should feed her. (Case 1)
*What should I feed her?*

Ok, now one by one, we're going to put the food back in the box. Laura, ask Joanne what to put back.
*Put back something*
(To Joanne): All right, Joanne, tell Laura what to put back.
                 (Put back the cucumber)
Laura, tell Joanne what to put back.
*The sandwich*

The next two examples are taken from children whose Rs are not as clear cut as the examples above. These two children did evidence some degree of distinction between *ask* and *tell* for case 3, but still they did not process the case 3 *ask* correctly. Their Rs to *tell* are correct, but with *ask* they are confused. The examples will illustrate their differing reactions.

Richard G., 9.2, interpreted *ask* correctly in the first case 3 instruction only, thereafter reverting to all *tell* interpretations. He is confused by this first instruction and answers first:

*What to feed the doll*

then immediately corrects himself to:

*What are we gonna feed the doll?*     (1 →)

This use of *we* instead of *I* is interesting, and we will find it with several other children at stage E below.

---

*Richard G., 9.2*

Tell Ann how many pencils there are here.

   *Three*

Can you tell her what color this crayon is.

   *Yellow*

I also want you to ask Ann some things. Will you ask her what color this book is.

   *What color's the book?*       (Blue)

Ask her what's in this box.

   *What's in the box?*       (Food)

M-hm. To feed the doll with. Now you did that very nicely, and you kept straight when you were supposed to ask or tell. Now you're going to do some more asking and telling, connected with feeding the doll. And first, I want you to ask Ann what to feed the doll.

1 →    *What to feed the doll . . . What are we gonna feed the doll?*     (Eggs)

(To Ann): Ann, will you tell Richard what to feed the doll.

          (Cucumber)

Richard, will you ask Ann what to feed the doll.

   *A sandwich*

Will you tell Ann what to feed the doll.

   *A hot dog*

And ask her what to feed the doll.

   *An apple*

Ask Ann what food to put back in the box.

   *Put the sandwich, this one*

(To Ann): Tell Richard what to put in the box.    (Eggs)

Ask Ann what to put in the box.

   *Cucumber*

Ask Ann what this is.

   *What's that?*       (Hot dog)

And ask Ann what to put in the box.
> *The apple*

(To Ann): Ann, tell Richard what to put in.
>                    (The sandwich)

And Richard, ask Ann what to put in.
> *The hot dog*

Will you ask Ann what color to make the square.
> *Make it green*

(To Ann): Ann, tell Richard what color to make the square.
>                         (Red)

Would you ask Ann her last name.
> *What's your last name?*          (Mulcahy)

Kim M., 9.7, has mixed Rs to the case 3 *ask* instructions, including three different Rs in all. Her first R is correct:
> *What should I feed the doll?*          (1 → )

The second time she tells (2 → ), and the third and fourth times, after some prodding, she resorts to the request form:
> *Would you put back the hot dog*          (3 → )
> *Would you make the square orange*          (4 → )

*Kim M., 9.7*

Tell Donald how many pencils there are here.
> *Three*

And would you tell Donald what color this tray is.
> *White*

And I want you to ask Donald some things, too, like ask Donald his last name.
> *What's your last name?*          (Morrell)

And would you ask Donald what time it is.
> *What time is it?*          (5 after 11)

And would you tell Donald what color that book is.
> *Blue*

And would you ask Donald what's in the box.
> *What's in the box?*          (I don't know)

Food. And now I'd like you to feed the doll, continuing with asking and telling. And would you first ask Donald what to feed the doll.

1 →    *What should I feed the doll?*          (Eggs)

And would you tell Donald what to feed the doll.
> *Cucumber*

Kim, would you ask Donald what to put back in the box.
2 → *Pear*
I think you told him that time. Listen carefully, *ask* Donald what to put back in the box.
3 → *Would you put back the hot dog*
And would you tell Donald what to put back in the box.
   *Bread*

Kim, would you ask Donald what color to make the square.
4 → *Would you make the square orange*
(To Donald): Would you tell Kim what color to make the triangle.                        (Black)

**4.3.9. Stage D. Success: Cases 1, 2, (3); Wrong Subject: Case 3**
6 children: boys: 6.10, 8.4, 8.8; girls: 6.9′, 7.0, 8.7

In stage D the children succeed at cases 1 and 2, and exhibit partial success with case 3. In this stage, we find for the first time that the children distinguish *ask* and *tell* for case 3. In response to the instructions containing *ask,* they ask a question. However, they assign the wrong subject to the complement verb. They assign a subject in accordance with the MDP, which gives the partner instead of the child to whom the instruction is addressed. They say:

Interviewer: Ask Barbara what to feed the doll.
Child: *What are you going to feed the doll?*

This is the stage we had originally set out to find, namely, that in which *ask* and *tell* are distinguished, but in which the exception to the MDP has not yet been learned. There were a variety of Rs given by the children in this stage, all questions, and all containing the subject *you.* The particular wording varied considerably. They are illustrated in the examples below.
   Steven B., 8.8, provided the most interesting and varied exchanges of all the stage D children. He used a different phraseology in each R, totaling six different forms in all (1–6 → ). Except for the R marked (3 → ) in the interview transcription which follows, when he does not understand, each question has *you* as subject:

   *What do you wanna feed the dog?*
   *Whadda ya feed the dog?*
   *What should you feed the dog?*
   *What are you supposed to put in the box?*
   *What are you gonna put in the box?*

*Steven B., 8.8*

First I want you to ask Lynn what to feed the dog.

1 → *What do you wanna feed the dog?*     (A hamburger)

And would you tell Lynn what to feed the dog next.

*I don't know. Peanut butter, I guess*

Now would you ask Lynn what to feed the dog.

2 → *Whadda ya feed the dog?*          (A pear)

(To Lynn): Will you tell Steven what to feed the dog.

(Mumble)

*That'll make him sick*

(To Lynn): Would you ask Steven what to feed the dog.

(The hot dog)

Would you ask Lynn what to feed the dog.

3 → *What to feed the dog?*

What's that mean?

4 → *I don't know. What should you feed the dog, then?*

Would you ask Lynn what food to put back in the box.

*Ah, ask Lynn to ask me to put it . . . what back in the box? Is that right?*

Ooh, that's a complicated one.

*I didn't understand you*

All right, I'll say it again. Ask Lynn what to put in the box.

5 → *Ok. What to put in the box. What are you supposed to put in the box?*          (Hamburger)

Tell Lynn what to put in the box.

*Eggs, I guess*

And ask Lynn what to put in the box.

6 → *What are you gonna put in the box?*     (Hot dog)

The next child, Steven V., 8.4, responded to the first case 3 *ask* instruction by telling (1 → ). With some prodding, he switched to asking for subsequent instructions (2–4 → ), and assigned the subject *you*. Notice that he remained unaffected by the correct model (5 → ).

*Steven V., 8.4*

Will you tell Bryan how many pencils there are here.

*Three*

Will you tell Bryan what color this crayon is.

*Yellow*

And I also want you to ask Bryan some things. Will you ask Bryan his last name.

*What is your last name, Bryan?*        (Burns)

And ask Bryan what time it is.

*What time is it?*        (I don't have my watch on)

Will you tell Bryan what color this book is.

*Blue*

Will you ask Bryan what's in this box.

*What's in the box?*        (Food. Want some?)

*She* wants some. Now the two of you are going to feed the doll. But I want you to do it by asking and telling some more. And first I'd like you to ask Bryan what to feed the doll.

1 →   *Mmm, I think a piece of bread over here*

Now will you tell Bryan what to feed the doll.

*I think those two eggs over there*

Steven, listen carefully, because I want you to *ask* Bryan something. I want you to ask him what to feed the doll.

2 →   *Feed, um, feed him, um, no . . . Do you know what to feed the doll?*

Now will you ask Bryan what food to put back in the box.

3 →   *What kind of food do you want to put back?*    (Hot dog)

(To Bryan): Bryan, ask Steven what to put back.

5 →        (Steven, what should I put back in the box?)

*Hamburg*

Steven, ask Bryan what to put back.

4 →   *Bryan, what do you want to put back in the box?*

(Hot dog. No, bread)

Ann M., 8.7, also gave varying Rs. Of the five key Rs, she assigned the subject *you* in four (1–3, 5 → ), and the subject *I* in one (4 → ). She too used different phraseology in her four Rs with subject *you:*

*What are you supposed to feed the doll?*
*What do you feed the doll?*
*What food do you put back in the box?*
*What color should you color the triangle?*

The Rs of this child, Ann M., appear to be instances of the impersonal use of the pronoun *you*. It is hard to tell whether she is closer to stage D or to stage E. However, her behavior indicated that she expected her partner to perform the action, and so we have placed her at stage D.

*Ann M., 8.7*

Tell Barbara how many pencils there are here.

 *Three*

Tell Barbara what color this crayon is.

 *Yellow*

And I also want you to *ask* Barbara some things. Would you ask her what color this book is.

 *What color's the book?*   (Blue)

Ask her what's in this box.

 *What's in the box?*   (Food)

All right. You did that fine, keeping straight whether you're supposed to ask or tell, and I'm going to have you do some more asking and telling connected with feeding the doll. You and Barbara are each going to feed the doll, and first, I want you to ask Barbara what to feed the doll.

1 → *What are you supposed to feed the doll?*  (Mumble)

Now will you tell Barbara what to feed the doll.

 *Eggs*

And again, ask Barbara what to feed the doll.

2 → *What do you feed the doll?*  (Hot dog)

And will you tell Barbara what to feed the doll.

 *Hamburger*

Now will you ask Barbara what food to put back in the box.

3 → *What food do you put in the box?*  (Eggs)

And Ann, would you ask Barbara what food you should put back in the box.

 *What should I put back in the box?*  (Hot dog)

And tell Barbara what she should put back in the box.

 *Hot dog*

And ask her what you should put back in the box.

 *What should I put back in the box?* (A pear)


Ann, ask Barbara what color to make the triangle.

4 → *What color should I color the triangle?*  (Green)

Tell Barbara what color to make the triangle.

 *Red*

Ann, ask Barbara what color to make the circle.

 *Blue*

Wait a minute. I said *ask* her. Ask her what color to make the circle.

5 → *What color should you color the circle?*  (Brown)

When you say, "What color should you color the circle," who are you thinking of doing the coloring?

> *I don't know*

I said to you, "Ask her what color to make the circle," and you said "What color should you color the circle." What did you mean? Who did you think was going to do it, you or Barbara?

> *Her*

Another borderline child that we have placed in stage D is Jimmy H., 6.10. He perhaps belongs in stage C. He does distinguish *ask* and *tell* for case 3, in that he responds correctly to *tell,* but indicates confusion with *ask.* To the *ask* instructions he always responds with a straight repetition of the complement clause:

Interviewer: Ask L what to feed the doll.
Child: *What to feed the doll*

Arrows ( → ) indicate these responses. The boxed section illustrates his lack of understanding of the construction.

> *Jimmy H., 6.10*
> First, I want you to ask Laura what to feed the doll.
> →     *What to feed the doll*        (Cucumber)
> Ask Laura what you should feed the doll.
>       *What should I feed the doll?*     (The hot dog)
> And ask Laura what to feed the doll.
> →     *What to feed the doll*     (Pear)

---

What do you mean when you say to her "What to feed the doll"? Who do you expect to do it when you say that? I don't exactly understand you.

> (Silence)

Say that again, what you said to her. *What to feed the doll.* Say it again.

> *What to feed the doll*

What's it mean?

> (Shrugs)

You're not sure?

> (Shakes his head)

You're just saying what I told you to say, without knowing what it means?

> (Nods)

---

I see. Tell Laura to stand up.
    *Stand up*
Ask her to sit down.
    *Sit down*
Tell her to put some food into the box.
    *Put some food into the box*
Tell her what to put into the box.
    *Put a tomato into the box*
Ask her what to put into the box.
→    *What to put in the box*    (The hot dog)
Ask her what you should put into the box.
    *What should I put into the box?*    (The bread)
Tell her what to put into the box.
    *Put the cucumber into the box*
Ask her what to put into the box.
    *What . . . ah . . . put the . . . ah, tomato in, well, put, ah, the hamburg in the box*

## 4.3.10. Stage E. Success: All Cases; Correct Subject: Case 3
14 children: boys: 5.10, 6.7, 7.3, 8.2, 9.7′, 9.7″, 9.8, 9.9; girls: 7.0′, 7.2, 8.6, 8.8′, 9.1, 9.8′

This is our final stage, and is characterized by success throughout. These children are able to respond correctly to all our constructions. To *ask* case 3 they respond:

Interviewer: Ask L what to feed the doll.
Child: *What should I feed the doll?*

Representative samples from interviews with three of the stage E children follow.

    *Lee R., 5.10*
First I want you to tell Lisa how many pencils there are here.
    *Three*
And I also want you to ask Lisa some things. Ask Lisa what's in this box.
    *What's in the box?*    (Some food)
Ask Lisa what time it is.
    *What time is it?*    (I don't know)
Tell Lisa what color this book is.
    *Blue*
And ask Lisa her last name.
    *What's your last name?*    (Vertuca)

Tell Lisa what color the tray is.

*White*

**Ok.** Let's bring out the food. It's mealtime. Now Lee, the doll is hungry, and the two of you are going to feed her. But I want you to do it in a special way, by asking and telling each other how. And I'll tell you each time what to do. Ok? First, Lee, will you tell Lisa what to feed her.

*The eggs*

(To Lisa): All right, Lisa, tell Lee what to feed her.

(The tomato)

Lee, ask Lisa what to feed her next.

*What should I feed her?* (The hamburger)

Lee, tell Lisa what to give her now.

*The toast*

And ask Lisa what to give her next.

*What should I give her?* (You should give her the hot dog)

Now piece by piece, we're gonna put the food back. Lee, ask Lisa what to put back first.

*What should I put back first?* (The toast)

Tell Lisa what to put back next.

*Put back the hot dog*

(To Lisa): Lisa, tell Lee what to put back. (Hamburger)

Lee, tell Lisa.

*Eggs*

Lee, ask Lisa what to put back next.

*The tomato*

Did you ask her or tell her?

*Tell her*

Ok, this time ask her what to put back.

*What should I put back?* (The cucumber)


*Alan H., 6.7*

I want you to tell Leon some things. Will you tell Leon how many pencils there are here.

*Three*

And tell Leon what color the tray is.

*White*

Now, I also want you to ask Leon some things. Will you ask Leon what color this book is.

*What color is the book?* (Blue)

And ask him what's in this box.

*What's in that box?* (Food)

All right, you can pour the food onto the tray.

    *I'll tell you which ones . . . oh, I like hamburgers, oh, no, I like eggs, some days I don't, not cucumbers, hot dogs, pears, toast, what's this? A roll.*

Hamburger, I think.

    *A hamburger in a roll. I love that*

All right, the two of you are going to feed the doll. In a special way. Alan, you'll either tell Leon what he should feed the doll, or you'll find out from Leon what you should feed the doll.

    *I'll tell Leon what to do*

Well, each time I'm going to tell you which way to go. Sometimes you'll ask him, and sometimes you'll tell him.

    *First can I try it by myself?*

All right, go ahead. Now, will you ask Leon what to feed the doll.

    *Leon, feed the doll these two eggs*

Tell Leon what to feed the doll.

    *Feed the doll a hamburg. No, that's not a hamburg*

All right, now, Alan, listen very carefully. Ask Leon what to feed the doll.

    *Tell him or ask him?*

Ask him.

    *What shall I feed the doll?*    (Hamburger)
    *That was already used*

That's all right. You can do it a second time. Very nice. Now tell him what to feed the doll.

    *Feed the doll a tomato*

Now, one by one, we're going to put the food back in the box. But in the same way. I want you to ask him sometimes, and tell him sometimes. Now first, will you ask him what to put back in the box.

    *What should I put back in the box?*  (Hamburger, hot dog)

Tell Leon what to put back in the box.

    *Leon, put in the cucumber*

(To Leon): Leon, tell Alan what to put back.    (Eggs)

(To Leon): Leon, ask Alan what to put back.    (Toast)

Well, all right. Good. Now you ask Leon what to put back.

    *What should I put back?*    (Tomato)


*Robin M., 9.8*

I want you to tell Caroline some things. Would you tell her how many pencils there are here.

    *Three*

Would you tell her what color this tray is.
>  *White*

And I want you to ask her some things, too. Would you ask her her last name.
>  *Carrie, what's your last name?*   (O'Connell)

Would you ask her what time it is.
>  *What time is it?*   (Quarter to 12)

Would you tell Caroline what color that book is.
>  *Blue*

Would you ask her what's in this box.
>  *What's in that box, Carrie?*   (Food)

Now, I want you to do some more asking and telling, connected with feeding the doll. And would you first ask Caroline what to feed the doll.
>  *Carrie, what should I feed the doll?*   (Eggs)

Now would you tell Caroline what to feed the doll. Tell Caroline what to feed the doll.
>  *Um, bread*

Ok. And again, would you ask Caroline what to feed the doll.
>  *What should I feed the doll, Carrie?*   (Hamburger)

Ok. Now we'll put the food away, and would you ask Caroline what to put back in the box.
>  *Carrie, what should I put in the box?*   (The tomato)

(To Caroline): And Caroline, would you ask Robin what to put in the box.   (What should I put in the box?)
>  *The pear*

Robin, tell Caroline what to put back next.
>  *The hamburger*

And ask her what to put back next.
>  *What should I put in the box?*   (The bread)

Will you ask Caroline what color to make the triangle.
>  *Carrie, what color should I make the triangle?*   (Blue)

Will you tell Caroline what color to make the square.
>  *Red*

Of our fourteen children in stage E, twelve answered as above, with no trouble. They knew what they were doing, and their competence was clear. The other two answered slightly differently, and are illustrated below.

Julianne S., 7.2, chose to assign the subject *we* instead of *I* in her Rs to case 3 *ask* instructions (2, 4, 5, →). We credited her with being

in stage E just the same, although notice that in her first R (1 →),
she assigns the subject *you*. She had no trouble assigning the subject
*I* when the instruction was case 1, which specifies the pronoun (3 →).

*Julianne S., 7.2*
First I want you to tell Richard some things. Will you tell
Richard how many pencils there are here.
> *There are three pencils here*

And will you tell Richard what color the crayon is.
> *Yellow*

And I also want you to ask Richard some things. Will you ask
Richard what color this book is.
> *What color is that book?*     (Blue)

And would you ask him what's in this box.
> *What's in that box?*     (Food)

Ok. You did very nicely, keeping straight whether you're supposed to ask or tell. And I'm going to have you do some more
asking and telling, connected with feeding the doll. Now, you
and Richard are both going to feed the doll, and first, I want you
to ask Richard what to feed the doll.

1 →  *Richard, what you gonna feed the doll?*   (The hot dog)

Now will you tell Richard what to feed the doll.
> *Richard, feed the doll the egg*

Now again, would you ask him what to feed the doll.

2 →  *Richard, what shall we feed the doll?*     (Hamburg)

And ask him what you should feed the doll.

3 →  *What should I feed the doll?*     (The cucumber)

Now tell him what food to put back in the box.
> *What food shall we put back in the box?*     (Cucumber)

And this time *tell* him what food to put back.
> *Put back the pear*

And ask him what to put back next.

4 →  *What shall we put back next?*

Juli, first will you ask Richard what color to make the triangle.

5 →  *Richard, what color shall we make the triangle?*   (Blue)

Tell Richard what color he should make the triangle.
> *Purple*

The next child, Caroline O., 9.1, used the subject *you* throughout
for *ask* case 3 (1–6 →). We have classified her in stage E because
she used the *you* as an impersonal (as did some children that we put

in stage **D**), but expected to carry out the action herself. As soon as she received an answer, she proceeded to perform the action. The following exchange is typical:

Interviewer: Ask Warren what to feed the doll.
Child: *What should you feed the doll?*   (Tomato)
(Caroline picks up the tomato and feeds the doll.)

She was asking to find out what *she* should do. This distinguished her from the stage **D** children, who asked to find out what the partner expected to do.

> *Caroline O., 9.1*
> Will you tell Warren how many pencils there are here.
> > *Three*
>
> And would you tell Warren what color the tray is.
> > *White*
>
> And I want you to ask Warren some things, too. Like, ask Warren his last name.
> > *What's your last name?*   (Hay)
>
> Ask Warren what time it is.
> > *What time is it?*   (23 past 11)
>
> And tell Warren what color the book is.
> > *Blue*
>
> And ask Warren what's in the box.
> > *What's in the box?*   (Food)
>
> Now you'll continue asking and telling and feed the doll. Caroline, would you first ask Warren what to feed the doll.
> 1 → *What should you feed the doll?*   (Tomato)
> > (Caroline did the feeding)
>
> Now would you tell Warren what to feed the doll.
> > *Eggs*
>
> And again, ask Warren what to feed the doll.
> > *Hamburger*
>
> Now you did it differently those two times. Listen to it. *Ask* Warren what to feed the doll.
> 2 → *What should you feed the doll?*
> Yeah, that's what you did the first time.
> (The bread with the peanut butter on it)
> (Caroline feeds the doll)
> Ask Warren what food to put back in the box.
> 3 → *What food should you put back in the box?*   (Cucumber)
> Caroline, ask Warren what to put back next.

4 →    *What should you put back next?*    (Hot dog)
And tell Warren what to put back.
*Bread*
And ask Warren what to put back.
5 →    *What should you put back?*    (Hamburger)

Caroline, would you ask Warren what color to make the triangle.
6 →    *What color should you make the triangle?*    (Orange)
And would you tell Warren what color to make the square.
*Yellow*

One final case is a child whose Rs give evidence of stages C, D, and E, all in the same interview. To the case 3 *ask* instructions, she responds once with the request form:
*Will you put the pear in the box.*    (1 →)
three times by telling (2 →), and three times by asking correctly (3 →). She is an excellent example of transition. Her interview follows.

*Lynn D., 8.10*
I want you to tell Richard some things. Will you tell Richard how many pencils there are here.
*Three*
And will you tell Richard what color this crayon is.
*Yellow*
And I also want you to *ask* Richard some things. Would you ask Richard what color this book is.
*What color is that book?*    (Blue)
And would you ask Richard what's in this box.
*What's in that box?*    (Food)
All right. Now you did that very nicely, keeping straight whether you were supposed to ask or tell. And I'm going to have you do some more asking and telling, connected with feeding the doll. And first, I want you to ask Richard what to feed the doll.
3 →    *Richard, what should I feed the doll?*    (Cucumber)
Go ahead. And would you tell Richard what to feed the doll.
*Hot dog*
And again, would you ask Richard what to feed the doll.
2 →    *Strawberry*
Now listen, because I'm saying *ask*. *Ask* Richard what to feed the doll.
3 →    *What . . . what should I feed the doll?*    (A pear)
Ask Richard which food to put back in the box.

3 → *What food should I put back in the box?*   (The apple)
And tell Richard what to put back in the box.
    *The piece of toast*
(To Richard): Richard, will you tell Lynn what to put in the box.   (The cucumber)
And will you ask Richard what to put in the box.
2 → *The boiled eggs*
Did you ask him or tell him?
    *Tell him*
This time would you *ask* him what to put in the box.
1 → *Will you put the pear in the box.*
Now ask him what *you* should put in the box.
    *What should I put in the box?*   (The hot dog)

Ask Richard what color to make the triangle.
2 → *Green*
(To Richard): And Richard, tell Lynn what color to make the triangle.   (Black)

Table 4.5 presents the forty children classified by stages, arranged in order by age within each stage.

**Table 4.5.** Classification of Children into *ask/tell* Differentiation Stages A–E. Descriptions of stages A (lowest) to E (highest) are given in Table 4.4. Stage A, group A: Children who answered consistently; Stage A, group A+: Children who answered inconsistently.

*Stage A.*   8 children
    Group A:   boys: 5.1, 5.2
              girls: 5.1', 5.3
    Group A+:   boys: 5.0, 5.3', 7.6
              girls: 7.1

*Stage B.*   2 children
    boy: 6.9
    girl: 6.6

*Stage C.*   9 children
    boys: 5.2', 5.3'', 7.9, 8.5, 9.2
    girls: 6.5, 6.5', 9.7, 10.0

*Stage D.*   6 children
    boys: 6.10, 8.4, 8.8   (C/D/E. g: 8.10)
    girls: 6.9', 7.0, 8.7

*Stage E.*   14 children
    boys: 5.10, 6.7, 7.3, 8.2, 9.7', 9.7'', 9.8, 9.9
    girls: 7.0', 7.2, 8.6, 8.8', 9.1, 9.8'

We wish now to take up another aspect of the difficulty experienced by the children in their interpretation of *ask*. We wish to discuss the possible effects of the particular form of the Ss presented to the children, namely, a command. The child was not asked simply to interpret a S, but rather he was required to carry out an instruction by saying something to his partner. There are several senses in which it is easier to tell than to ask under such circumstances, and these factors may have contributed somewhat to the children's difficulties. For one thing, there is very likely less effort involved in formulating a one-word answer than in doing the grammatical work of generating a question. It may be simply easier to say BLUE than to manage WHAT COLOR'S THAT BOOK?, and this may have been playing a role. Second, given the interview situation, it is likely that one expects to give out information, not to ask for it, and the children may have been hampered by this fairly natural expectation. Third, there is the interpersonal situation to consider, and the role that the child is playing with respect to the interviewer and to his partner. The child is at first an addressee, when he receives the instruction. He becomes an addresser in responding to it. If he tells, things stop there. We may diagram it thus:

| *Interviewer* | | *Child* | | *Partner* |
|---|---|---|---|---|
| ADDRESSER | → | ADDRESSEE | | |
| | | ↓ | | |
| | | ADDRESSER | → | ADDRESSEE |

In order to tell, the child simply effects one change of role, from addressee to addresser. However, in order to ask, he must require of his partner to become an addresser, and must reassume the role of addressee, this time in relation to a second party. The *ask* diagram looks like this:

| *Interviewer* | | *Child* | | *Partner* |
|---|---|---|---|---|
| ADDRESSER | → | ADDRESSEE | | |
| | | ↓ | | |
| | | ADDRESSER | → | ADDRESSEE |
| | | | | ↓ |
| | | ADDRESSEE | ← | ADDRESSER |

The child must change from addressee to addresser, and back to addressee again.

All of these factors may be contributing to the child's observed difficulties in asking in our test situation. The significance of their role, however, does not extend to the different degrees of difficulty observed between simple and complex constructions, since these factors are held constant for all our constructions. Their effect may be to increase overall difficulty, but they should be unrelated to the sequence of stages evidenced by the children.

In an attempt to overcome the complications inherent in the 'command' situation, we ran a second experiment with different children in which we presented pairs of pictures (Figures 4.4, 4.5, and 4.6) to the children and asked them to select the picture which correctly represented a test S. We tested only case 3 with these pictures, and used three Ss:

(58) The boy asks the girl what shoes to wear.
(59) The girl asks the boy what to paint.
(60) The girl asks the boy which juice to drink.

These pictures are presented on the following page. The first of each pair (1a, 2a, 3a) illustrates the correct *ask* interpretation, complement subject same as main clause subject:

1a. boy asks: *What shoes should I wear?*
2a. girl asks: *What should I paint?*
3a. girl asks: *Which juice should I drink?*

The second picture of each pair (1b, 2b, 3b) illustrates the *tell* interpretation:

1b. boy tells: *Wear those shoes*
2b. girl tells: *Paint a dog*
3b. girl tells: *Drink that juice*

and also the incorrect *ask* interpretation, complement subject same as main clause object:

1b. boy asks: *What shoes are you going to wear?*
2b. girl asks: *What are you going to paint?*
3b. girl asks: *Which juice are you going to drink?*

The child was instructed to look at both pictures of a pair, and to select the one which showed what the test S said. We then read him the test S. After he made his choice, he was asked to tell what the boy (or girl) in the picture was saying. The latter two interpretations (*tell,* and *ask* with wrong subject) which both led the child to select picture (b) were differentiated when the child quoted the picture boy or girl.

**Figure 4.4.** Test Pictures 1a (left), Correct Interpretation, and 1b (right), Incorrect Interpretation. Test sentence: The boy asks the girl what shoes to wear. Subject is shown both pictures simultaneously and asked: 1. Which picture shows the boy asking the girl what shoes to wear? 2. (after selection) What is he saying to her?

**Figure 4.5.** Test Pictures 2a (left), Correct Interpretation, and 2b (right), Incorrect Interpretation. Test sentence: The girl asks the boy what to paint. Subject is shown both pictures simultaneously and asked: 1. Which picture shows the girl asking the boy what to paint? 2. (after selection) What is she saying to him?

**Figure 4.6.** Test Pictures 3a (left), Correct Interpretation, and 3b (right), Incorrect Interpretation. Test sentence: The girl asks the boy which juice to drink. Subject is shown both pictures simultaneously and asked: 1. Which picture shows the girl asking the boy which juice to drink? 2. (after selection) What is she saying to him?

We tested fifteen new children from two other schools, five each from grades 1, 2, and 3. Prior to giving the child the picture test, we determined what stage he belonged to according to our command interview. For both the interview and the pictures, he was scored according to his best response. Our comparison of the two sets of results showed that of our fifteen children, nine did the same on the pictures as on the commands, five did better on the pictures, and one did worse. The children who did better moved up one stage with the pictures, and the one child who did worse moved down one stage. We were measuring with a different approach that some children found easier to comprehend. Since the pictures illustrated only case 3, they proved excellent for distinguishing among stages C, D, and E. Cases 1 and 2 do not lend themselves to illustration, and cannot so easily be explored with pictures.

Before closing this *ask/tell* section, we would like to raise a question concerning our case 3 construction:

Ask L what to feed the doll.

We found 9-year-olds and 10-year-olds who could not, even with prodding, respond with the correct answer:

*What should I feed the doll?*

The question that we wish to raise is whether these children are still in a process of acquisition with respect to this structure and will at some future time be able to interpret it correctly, or whether perhaps they may already have reached what for them constitutes adult competence. We have observed from informal questioning that this structure is a problematic one for many adults, and that there are many adult speakers who persist in assigning the wrong subject to the complement verb. This seems to be a structure that is never properly learned by a substantial number of speakers. This kind of imperfect learning of one's native language has been commented on by Bloomfield (1927) with respect to Menomini:[9]

In inflection, Menomini, like the other Algonquian languages, has an *obviative* form for subsidiary third persons. Thus, if our story is of a man meeting another man and of the ensuing occurrences, our first man will be spoken of in the normal third person form, and the other man in the obviative form. The good Menomini speaker has no such difficulty as we have with our single pronoun *he*. But bad Menomini speakers profit not at all from this distinction, but get as tangled in their two forms as a bad speaker of English with his one ambiguous *he*.

9. Bloomfield (1964), p. 396.

Similarly, we have found that many adults are getting tangled in their complement subject assignment in our test construction following *ask*. What this means in terms of our 9-year-olds and 10-year-olds who have not reached stage E is hard to know. Perhaps they have reached adult competence for this structure, perhaps not. Some of them will almost certainly remain at stage D. Perhaps there is a critical learning period during which deliberate exposure to these constructions could result in acquisition which otherwise might never take place for certain children. These questions ought to be explored in future studies. Of greatest relevance for this study would be a statistical check on adult errors as compared with errors observed in children from 9 to 10 up into adulthood.

### 4.4. Pronominalization

**Interview**

*Initial setting up:* Place on the table in front of the child the figures of Mickey Mouse and Pluto Pup.

*Interview:*
1. *Introduction*
   Who is this?      (Indicate Mickey Mouse)
   And who is this?      (Indicate Pluto Pup)
2. *Practice*
   I'm going to tell you some things about Mickey Mouse and Pluto, like
   Mickey wants to go to the movies.     or
   Pluto is tired.
   And I want you to tell me each time who it is that I talked about. Like, if I say:
   Mickey wants to go to the movies,
   And I ask you:
   Who wants to go to the movies?
   What would you answer?
   Suppose I say: Pluto is tired.
   Can you tell me who is tired?
   Now how about: Pluto knew that Mickey was tired.
       Who was tired?
       And who knew it?

And, Mickey told his mother he was hungry.
>Who was hungry?
>And who told his mother?

All right, you've got the idea. Here we go with some more.

3. *Test sentences*

Pluto thinks he knows everything.
>Pluto thinks that *who* knows everything?

He found out that Mickey won the race.
>Who found out?
>And who won the race?

After he got the candy, Mickey left.
>Who got the candy?
>And who left?

Before he went out, Pluto took a nap.
>Before *who* went out?
>And who took the nap?

He didn't know why Pluto felt so sad.
>Who didn't know?
>And who felt sad?

Mickey yawned when he sat down.
>When *who* sat down?

He was glad that Mickey got the candy.
>Who was glad?

If he wins the race, Pluto will be happy.
>If *who* wins the race?

He was 5 years old when Pluto broke his leg.
>Who was 5 years old?
>And who broke his leg?

Mickey said that he was hungry for a big dinner.
>Who was hungry?

When he was 7, Mickey learned to throw a ball.
>When *who* was 7?

He thinks Pluto knows how.
>Who thinks?

Mickey knew that he was going to be late.
>Who was going to be late?
>And who knew it?

When he changed schools, Pluto was 8 years old.
>When *who* changed schools?

Pluto thinks he's going to win the race.
>Who's going to win the race?

## Discussion

*Test Construction:* (D) Pronominalization

*Nature of complexity:* Restrictions on a grammatical operation apply under certain limited conditions only.

In this interview the child's interpretation of pronominal reference in three different structures is tested:

STRUCTURE 1: *pronoun is in main clause, precedes NP*
Sample S, type 1: He found out that Mickey won the race.
STRUCTURE 2: *pronoun is in subordinate clause, precedes NP*
Sample S, type 2: After he got the candy, Mickey left.
STRUCTURE 3: *pronoun is in subordinate clause, follows NP*
Sample S, type 3: Pluto thinks he knows everything.

In Ss of type 1, the pronoun must refer to someone else outside the S (restricted reference, nonidentity requirement), whereas in types 2 and 3 it may refer either to the occurring NP or to someone else (unrestricted reference). Our purpose is to determine whether the child knows that there is a nonidentity requirement for Ss of type 1, as contrasted with 2 and 3, which have no such requirement.

We presented the child with five Ss of each type. The fifteen Ss used were:

*Type 1*    (Nonidentity requirement)
1. He found out that Mickey won the race.
2. He didn't know why Pluto felt so sad.
3. He was glad that Mickey got the candy.
4. He was 5 years old when Pluto broke his leg.
5. He thinks Pluto knows how.

*Type 2*    (Unrestricted reference)
6. After he got the candy, Mickey left.
7. Before he went out, Pluto took a nap.
8. If he wins the race, Pluto will be very happy.
9. When he was 7, Mickey learned to throw a ball.
10. When he changed schools, Pluto was 8 years old.

*Type 3*    (Unrestricted reference)
11. Pluto thinks he knows everything.
12. Mickey yawned when he sat down.
13. Mickey said that he was hungry for a big dinner.

14. Mickey knew that he was going to be late.
15. Pluto thinks he's going to win the race.

These Ss were presented to the children in scrambled order, as shown in the interview at the beginning of this section.

The interview procedure was as follows. We placed before the child two figures, Mickey Mouse and Pluto Pup, and had him identify them. We explained to him that we were going to tell him some things about Mickey and Pluto, and then ask him some questions to see if he could tell who we were talking about. We then gave him some examples for practice. The first few practice Ss contained no instances of pronominalization, and named only one figure:

Mickey wants to go to the movies.
    Who wants to go to the movies?
Pluto is tired.
    Who is tired?

The next practice S named both figures:

Pluto knew that Mickey was tired.
    Who was tired?
    Who knew it?

The final practice S contained a pronoun:

Mickey told his mother he was hungry.
    Who was hungry?
    And who told his mother?

When we were sure that the child understood the task, we proceeded to the test Ss. For the first few test Ss, we asked him not only about the pronoun, but also about the NP, just to check that he was really listening and able to report meaningfully. Several times later on in the interview we again checked on the NP as well as the pronoun. If a child erred in reporting on the NP, we stopped and repeated the S, and pointed out to him the discrepancy. He was then able to correct himself and proceed. Any time a child requested a repetition of a S, or hesitated for a long time, we read the S again.

The course of the interview was a smooth one. The children were able to understand readily what we meant and what they were supposed to do. The task of answering the questions was simplified for them by the use of the figures, which provided a physical object to focus on while they considered the Ss. During our preliminary questioning with neighborhood children we found that holding the S in mind and thinking about it abstractly was difficult for many children, and we did not really trust the answers they were giving. Under normal circumstances of language use, a pronoun which refers outside of a S refers to someone named in an earlier S, not to an abstract 'someone else.' In the absence of context or preceding Ss, our figures helped to provide the 'someone else.' Having the actual figures of Mickey Mouse and Pluto standing on the table in front of them helped the children enormously. They really used the figures, and many preferred to point to their choice, or pick up the figure, rather than answer with the figure's name. They watched the figures while we read the S, and then when we asked the question, their eyes moved to the figure of their choice. Naming the figure was almost superfluous — their eyes told the whole story. Several times it happened that a child looked at one figure and named the other. When this happened, we stopped and asked him, "Now who do you mean, because you're looking at Pluto but you said Mickey." "No," was the answer, "I mean *him,* Pluto." They invariably meant the one they were looking at. Sometimes a child would have trouble deciding, and his eyes would shift back and forth from Mickey to Pluto. When this happened, we repeated the S, and this usually helped him to come to a decision.

Except for the above situation in which a moment's discussion cleared up the confusion, we accepted the child's first response to each S as final. The only time we rechecked any Ss was when the child gave identity (incorrect) Rs for any of the type 1 Ss. To make sure that these errors were not just slips, of particular importance when there was only one such R out of the five, we went back at the end of the interview and repeated several of the type 1 Ss, including the originally incorrect ones. Second Rs almost always matched first Rs, indicating that this was really the way the child understood the S, or at least that his first R was indeed a reliable possibility for him. The important fact about the repetitions was that no child corrected his score to perfect on the second round, but all retained some identity Rs. We concluded on this basis that the first Rs were significant indicators of the child's interpretations, and our results in Table 4.6 below show first Rs only.

The question arises as to whether the particular Ss used prejudiced the children's Rs in some way. The type 1 Ss were the only ones for which a R could be incorrect, and the distribution of Rs to these shows that no individual S is guilty of eliciting a disproportionate number of identity Rs. The identity Rs were scattered among the Ss, as can be seen in Table 4.6.

Normally this pronominalization test was given last in the interview, after the other three constructions had been completed. Some of the kindergarteners appeared to tire, however, by the time we reached this point in the interview, and we thought it best for these children to postpone the pronominalization questioning until another day. When we saw that a child could not comfortably go on, we terminated the interview and sent him back to class. Twenty minutes of concentration on verbal tasks had been enough. On our next trip to the school we called him back just for the pronominalization questions. This happened with three children, ages 5.2, 5.3′, and 5.3″. Of course, they were better able to cooperate when starting fresh, although this did not seem to affect their scores. The three children who were called back and did the task first were among those who failed (see 5.2, 5.3′, and 5.3″ in Group A, Table 4.6); and among those who succeeded were two 5-year-olds who did the task at the end of their half-hour (see 5.2′ and 5.10 in Group B, Table 4.6). Apparently these children's ability to deal with pronominal reference in the test Ss was not affected by freshness in approaching the task.

Table 4.6 gives the children's Rs to the test Ss. The children are grouped according to their Rs to the type 1 Ss: Group A comprises those children who misinterpreted one or more of the type 1 Ss, and Group B comprises those who gave only correct interpretations to the type 1 Ss. A+ indicates an identity R, i.e., that the child identified the pronoun as the figure named elsewhere in the S, and a— indicates a nonidentity R, i.e., that the child identified the pronoun as the figure not named in the S.

The Rs that are significant in Table 4.6 are the incorrect Rs to type 1 Ss, which were exhibited by 9 of the children. These Rs appear in the upper left of Table 4.6, Group A. For these children, we conclude that pronominal reference is unrestricted for this construction as yet. The children wrongly reported identity of pronoun with NP for one, two, or three of the Ss, with considerable variation of Ss misinterpreted. We cannot conclude on the basis of this one construction that these children are unaware that a nonidentity requirement exists in their language in general, but we can say that they do not know to apply it to this test construction. Since this construction is one of the simplest and clearest examples of the nonidentity requirement, however, the evidence strongly suggests that these children have in fact not yet acquired knowledge of this restriction.

Group B contains the children who gave only correct Rs to type 1 Ss. The fact that these children gave no identity Rs to the type 1 Ss

**Table 4.6.** Children's Judgments of Pronominal Reference in 3 Sentence Types.

| | Age of child | Type 1 Ss | | | | | Type 2 Ss | | | | | Type 3 Ss | | | | |
|---|---|---|---|---|---|---|---|---|---|---|---|---|---|---|---|---|
| | | 1 | 2 | 3 | 4 | 5 | 6 | 7 | 8 | 9 | 10 | 11 | 12 | 13 | 14 | 15 |
| Group A Incorrect | 5.0 | + | − | − | − | + | + | − | − | + | − | + | + | − | + | + |
| | 5.1 | − | − | + | + | − | − | + | − | − | − | + | + | + | + | − |
| | *5.1' | + | + | − | − | − | + | − | − | − | − | + | + | + | + | + |
| | 5.2 | − | − | + | + | + | − | + | + | + | − | + | + | − | + | + |
| | *5.3 | + | − | + | − | − | + | + | − | + | + | + | + | + | + | + |
| | 5.3' | − | − | + | − | − | − | − | − | + | − | + | − | + | + | + |
| | 5.3'' | − | − | + | + | − | − | + | − | + | − | − | + | + | + | + |
| | 6.10 | + | − | − | − | − | − | − | − | + | − | − | + | − | + | − |
| | *8.10 | − | − | − | + | − | − | − | − | + | − | + | + | − | + | + |
| Group B Correct | 5.2' | − | − | − | − | − | − | − | − | + | − | − | + | − | + | − |
| | 5.10 | − | − | − | − | − | − | + | − | + | − | + | + | + | + | + |
| | *6.5 | − | − | − | − | − | − | − | − | − | − | + | + | + | + | + |
| | *6.5' | − | − | − | − | − | − | − | − | + | − | + | + | + | + | − |
| | *6.6 | − | − | − | − | − | − | − | − | − | − | + | + | + | − | + |
| | 6.7 | − | − | − | − | − | − | + | − | − | − | + | + | + | + | + |
| | 6.9 | − | − | − | − | − | − | + | − | + | − | + | + | + | + | + |
| | *6.9' | − | − | − | − | − | + | + | − | + | − | + | + | + | − | + |
| | *7.0 | − | − | − | − | − | − | − | − | − | − | + | + | + | + | + |
| | *7.0' | − | − | − | − | − | − | − | − | − | − | + | + | + | + | + |
| | *7.1 | − | − | − | − | − | − | − | − | + | − | + | + | + | + | − |
| | *7.2 | − | − | − | − | − | − | + | − | + | − | + | + | + | + | + |
| | 7.3 | − | − | − | − | − | − | + | − | − | − | + | − | + | + | + |
| | 7.6 | − | − | − | − | − | + | + | − | − | + | + | − | − | − | + |
| | 7.9 | − | − | − | − | − | − | + | − | + | + | + | + | + | − | + |
| | 8.2 | − | − | − | − | − | + | + | − | + | − | + | + | + | + | + |
| | 8.4 | − | − | − | − | − | + | + | − | + | − | + | + | + | + | + |
| | 8.5 | − | − | − | − | − | − | + | − | − | + | + | + | + | + | + |
| | *8.6 | − | − | − | − | − | − | + | − | + | + | + | + | + | + | + |
| | *8.7 | − | − | − | − | − | − | − | − | + | − | + | + | + | + | + |
| | 8.8 | − | − | − | − | − | − | − | − | + | − | + | + | + | − | + |
| | *8.8' | − | − | − | − | − | − | + | − | + | − | + | + | + | + | + |
| | *9.1 | − | − | − | − | − | − | − | − | + | + | + | + | + | + | + |
| | 9.2 | − | − | − | − | − | + | + | − | + | − | + | + | − | + | + |
| | *9.7 | − | − | − | − | − | − | − | − | + | + | − | + | + | + | − |
| | 9.7' | − | − | − | − | − | + | + | − | + | − | + | − | + | − | + |
| | 9.7'' | − | − | − | − | − | + | − | + | + | − | − | + | + | + | − |
| | 9.8 | − | − | − | − | − | + | + | + | + | + | + | − | + | + | + |
| | *9.8' | − | − | − | − | − | − | + | − | − | − | + | − | + | + | + |
| | 9.9 | − | − | − | − | − | + | + | + | − | − | + | − | + | + | + |
| | *10.0 | − | − | − | − | − | − | + | − | + | − | + | + | + | − | + |

Type 1 S: He knew that Pluto was sad. Type 2 S: If he wins, Pluto will be happy. Type 3 S: Mickey said he was hungry. The 15 test sentences used are listed on p. 104. + = identity of pronoun with NP; − = nonidentity of pronoun with NP.

Children under 6 exhibit ignorance of nonidentity requirement for type 1 Ss (+s in upper left box, Group A). Responses of children over 6 are restricted to nonidentity for type 1 Ss (−s in lower left box, Group B). Responses of both groups are unrestricted for Ss of types 2 and 3 (+s and −s in remaining boxes). Ages of girls are preceded by asterisk (*5.3).

is not proof that they know the restriction. We would need a more far-reaching study to substantiate such a claim. From our data we can say only that the Group B children have given us no evidence to the contrary, i.e., they have not demonstrated that they do *not* know the restriction, as have the children in Group A. We can only consider it highly likely that they do in fact know the nonidentity requirement.

The other two constructions, types 2 and 3, allow unrestricted reference, and consequently there can be no scoring of correct and incorrect Rs. Since both references are permitted, all answers are correct. There were more identity Rs for type 3 than for type 2, which is to be expected in line with adult judgments of the constructions. The data are too few to make generalizations, but it is interesting to note that three of the children, from these few Ss at least, appear to have a very simple system indeed. Ages 6.5, 7.0, and 7.0′ interpret all preceding pronouns with nonidentity, and all following ones with identity. They seem to be operating with the simple principle that the basic function of a pronoun is to refer to what precedes, without further refinements.

The children's errors in this pronominalization interview are more closely correlated with age than were those in the other three interviews that we conducted. With only three exceptions (ages 6.10, 8.10, and 5.2), the age cutoff between correct and incorrect Rs is approximately 5.6. If our small sample is representative, then this seems to be a fact about his language that a child learns with considerable regularity at about age 5 or 6. We do not find here the variety in age of acquisition that we found with the other constructions that we tested. Rather the principles of pronominalization appear to be acquired by the majority of children at about the same age. Our conjecture about the reasons underlying this difference is that the rules for pronominal reference are considerably more basic and more general than the rules underlying our other constructions. The rules for *promise* and *ask* are specific ones, applying to a particular word. The rule for *easy to see* is of a more general structural nature, but again pertains to, or is signaled by, the word *easy* and others of its class.

The rules for pronominal reference are qualitatively different. They pertain to no specific word or class of words, but derive from principles which apply to whole Ss, very generally, on the basis of their structure. In order to learn them the child must deal with a general principle, rather than with lexical exceptions. We may speculate that perhaps it is this difference which accounts for their more regularized acquisition. Since a basic principle of the language is involved, rather than a fact relating to a specific lexical item or class of items, the child may acquire it at a certain maturational level. It is perhaps as if pronominalization is a basic tool of the language, whereas our other constructions are specialized skills. Children may become equipped to handle the basic tools at a certain stage in their maturation, whereas the timing of acquisition of specialized constructions is dependent on other factors, perhaps such as degree of linguistic elaboration in their environment, intelligence, rate of general cognitive development, and so on. We do not really know what factors influence these differing rates of acquisition for these other structures, but our results indicate that the principles of pronominalization, at least, seem not to be subject to the same influences.

We would like to consider also the reactions of the children to what they were doing in this interview. What follows is highly speculative, but perhaps will be of interest to some readers, and perhaps is indicative of an aspect of the children's competence. The older ones enjoyed the task much more than the younger ones did. The younger ones reacted as if the whole thing was sort of pointless and a bit of an imposition. Of course this was the last interview of the four, and the younger children were more tired by this time. However, we do attribute this difference in reaction of the younger and older children to something more than just fatigue. Even when this interview came first, as when the child was called back a second time, the younger children still were more bored with it than the older ones were. There seemed to us to be a real difference in the degree to which they felt imposed upon. The task was simply less interesting to them, and this we interpreted as a result of the extent of their proficiency.

The older ones were well aware that in some Ss the answer had to be one way, and that in other Ss they had a choice. Some of the older children answered sometimes, for the unrestricted constructions, "It could be either one." The problem for them was an intriguing one because they were aware of the possibilities and recognized the surprising fact of restriction when it occurred. One is not normally aware, certainly, of the fact that in some Ss *he* has to be 'somebody else.' When one is asked to make this kind of judgment, and thinks about what *he* refers to, it is something of a surprise to find that this is so. This degree of awareness renders the task interesting. The child is busy exercising a skill, and he sees a point to what he is doing. The younger children seemed to view the task as purely arbitrary. They were willing enough to cooperate and answer the questions, but they did not seem to see any point to it all. Not only the children in Group A gave us this impression, but also the younger ones in Group B. For the younger ones in B, perhaps the feeling of exercising a skill was absent. The 'skill' itself was perhaps less clearly defined than in the case of the older children, and their awareness of the different status of *he* was lower. Under these circumstances, getting through fifteen Ss was more of a nuisance to the child. We have brought this up for this interview because the difference in reactions was so striking. This was not the case for the other interviews, in which all the children evidenced interest and involvement, and usually even enjoyment.

# 5 Discussion

In this section we would like to correlate the results from the four constructions tested, and point out some general trends that our data suggest.

The performance of each child on all four tests is presented in Table 5.1 with the children listed by age. These performance scores are derived from our data of Chapter 4 as follows. For *ask/tell,* the stage is indicated directly, from A (lowest) to E (highest), according to the characterization of stages in §4(C). For the other three tests, the child is scored simply as 'correct' (+), or 'incorrect' (−). For *promise* this entails a reduction of the four stages described in §4(B) to two: 'correct' comprises the better two *promise* stages of §4(B), and 'incorrect' comprises the poorer two. For *easy to see,* the correct/incorrect representation is the same as in §4(A). For pronominalization, 'correct' comprises the children who made no errors (Group B), and 'incorrect' comprises the children who did make errors (Group A). These scores as represented in Table 5.1 will be used as the basis of our discussion in this section.

Table 5.2 presents the same data, with the children listed separately for each construction, again by age.

We will first consider the results for each construction separately, and point out several interesting differences in the process of acquisition evidenced by the children with respect to the different structures. We will then proceed to an analysis of the coordinated data.

For *ask/tell*, we find a wide distribution of stages among the children in our sample, indicating considerable variation in age of

112

**Table 5.1.** Children's Performances on Four Test Constructions, Listed According to Age of Child. In *ask/tell* stage, A = lowest and E = highest. + = correct; − = incorrect. Ages of children are given in years and months (5.2 = 5 years, 2 months). Girls are indicated by asterisks (*5.3).

| Age | Ask/Tell stage | Promise | Easy to see | Pronominalization |
|-----|----------------|---------|-------------|-------------------|
| 5.0 | A+ | − | − | − |
| 5.1 | A | − | − | − |
| *5.1' | A | − | − | − |
| 5.2 | A | + | − | − |
| 5.2' | C | + | + | + |
| *5.3 | A | − | − | − |
| 5.3' | A+ | − | − | − |
| 5.3" | C | + | − | − |
| 5.10 | E | + | + | + |
| *6.5 | C | − | − | + |
| *6.5' | C | + | + | + |
| *6.6 | B | − | − | + |
| 6.7 | E | + | + | + |
| 6.9 | B | − | − | + |
| *6.9' | D | − | + | + |
| 6.10 | D | − | − | − |
| *7.0 | D | + | + | + |
| *7.0' | E | + | + | + |
| *7.1 | A+ | − | + | + |
| *7.2 | E | + | + | + |
| 7.3 | E | + | + | + |
| 7.6 | A+ | − | − | + |
| 7.9 | C | + | + | + |
| 8.2 | E | + | − | + |
| 8.4 | D | + | + | + |
| 8.5 | C | + | − | + |
| *8.6 | E | + | + | + |
| *8.7 | D | − | + | + |
| 8.8 | D | + | + | + |
| *8.8' | E | + | + | + |
| *8.10 | C/D/E | − | + | − |
| *9.1 | E | + | + | + |
| 9.2 | C | + | + | + |
| *9.7 | C | + | + | + |
| 9.7' | E | + | + | + |
| 9.7" | E | + | + | + |
| 9.8 | E | + | + | + |
| *9.8' | E | + | + | + |
| 9.9 | E | + | + | + |
| *10.0 | C | + | + | + |

**Table 5.2.** Children's Performance on Four Test Constructions, with Children Listed Separately by Age for Each Construction.

| Ask-Tell stages | | | | | Promise | | Easy to see | | Pronominalization | |
|---|---|---|---|---|---|---|---|---|---|---|
| A | B | C | D | E | Incorrect | Correct | Incorrect | Correct | Incorrect | Correct |
| 5.0 | *6.6 | 5.2' | *6.9' | 5.10 | 5.0 | 5.2 | 5.0 | 5.2' | 5.0 | 5.2' |
| 5.1 | 6.9 | 5.3" | 6.10 | 6.7 | 5.1 | 5.2' | 5.1 | 5.10 | 5.1 | 5.10 |
| *5.1' | | *6.5 | *7.0 | *7.0' | *5.1' | 5.3' | *5.1' | *6.5' | *5.1' | *6.5 |
| 5.2 | | *6.5' | 8.4 | *7.2 | *5.3 | 5.10 | 5.2 | 6.7 | 5.2 | *6.5' |
| *5.3 | | 7.9 | *8.7 | 7.3 | 5.3' | *6.5' | *5.3 | *6.9' | *5.3 | *6.6 |
| 5.3' | | 8.5 | 8.8 | 8.2 | *6.5 | 6.7 | 5.3' | *7.0 | 5.3' | 6.7 |
| *7.1 | | *8.10 | | *8.6 | *6.6 | *7.0 | 5.3" | *7.0' | 5.3" | 6.9 |
| 7.6 | | 9.2 | | *8.8' | 6.9 | *7.0' | *6.5 | 7.1 | 6.10 | *6.9' |
| | | *9.7 | | *9.1 | *6.9' | *7.2 | *6.6 | *7.2 | *8.10 | *7.0 |
| | | *10.0 | | 9.7' | 6.10 | 7.3 | 6.9 | 7.3 | | *7.0' |
| | | | | 9.7" | *7.1 | 7.9 | 6.10 | 7.9 | | *7.1 |
| | | | | 9.8 | 7.6 | 8.2 | 7.6 | 8.4 | | *7.2 |
| | | | | *9.8' | *8.7 | 8.4 | 8.2 | *8.6 | | 7.3 |
| | | | | 9.9 | *8.10 | 8.5 | 8.5 | 8.7 | | 7.6 |
| | | | | | | *8.6 | | 8.8 | | 7.9 |
| | | | | | | 8.8 | | *8.8' | | 8.2 |
| | | | | | | *8.8' | | *8.10 | | 8.4 |
| | | | | | | *9.1 | | *9.1 | | 8.5 |
| | | | | | | 9.2 | | 9.2 | | *8.6 |
| | | | | | | *9.7 | | *9.7 | | *8.7 |
| | | | | | | 9.7' | | 9.7 | | 8.8 |
| | | | | | | 9.7" | | 9.7" | | *8.8' |
| | | | | | | 9.8 | | 9.8 | | *9.1 |
| | | | | | | *9.8' | | *9.8' | | 9.2 |
| | | | | | | 9.9 | | 9.9 | | 9.7 |
| | | | | | | *10.0 | | *10.0 | | 9.7' |
| | | | | | | | | | | 9.7" |
| | | | | | | | | | | 9.8 |
| | | | | | | | | | | *9.8' |
| | | | | | | | | | | 9.9 |
| | | | | | | | | | | *10.0 |

acquisition of these structures (refer to Table 5.1). Although the general pattern is one of gradual improvement with increase in age, the high degree of individual variation indicates a strong dependence of this acquisition on individual rate of development. The overall picture shows that the 5-year-olds are predominantly at stage A, the 6s, 7s, and 8s evidence all the stages from A to E, and the 9s are predominantly at stage E. However, the degree of variation from this overall pattern is such that we find children as young as 5.10 who have already reached stage E, and children up to the age of 7.6 who are still in stage A. Stage C appears at all ages, from the very youngest (two 5-year-olds) to the very oldest children in our sample (two 9s and a 10-year-old). The 6s, 7s and 8s who evidence all the stages do so in a very mixed fashion, with stages C, D, and E all represented at each age. Moreover, what is surprising is that we do not find an age in our sample beyond which the children are reliably in stage E. Stage C is still well represented among our oldest children: one third of the children from age 9 on are still in stage C. Apparently we must go to still older children to find a resolution of this problem.[10] The dominant features of the acquisition of this structure, particularly as contrasted with our other constructions (as will be seen below) seem to be first, variability in age of acquisition and strong correlation with individual rate of development, and second, persistence of errors up through the oldest children tested.

The next two constructions, *promise* and *easy to see,* show characteristics similar to each other and will be discussed together. If we scan down the middle two columns of Table 5.1 we see that at the top the −s predominate, then comes a central section of mixed −s and +s, and finally near the bottom, all +s. This means simply that the youngest children fairly consistently do not know the construction, the 6s, 7s, and 8s are mixed, and the 9s all know the construction. For *promise,* we find only +s from 9 on; for *easy to see,* from 8.6 on. What is important here is that these two constructions share the following pattern. Beyond a certain age all children know the construction. Prior to this age, the children are mixed. What we find prior to this age is a fairly lengthy period in which a child may or may not have learned the construction, depending on his rate of development. This 'potential learning' period, the period of mixed +s and −s, in our data is as long as three or four years. For *promise,* it extends from age 5.2 to 8.10. For *easy to see,* it is from

10. See §4(C) for a discussion of the possibility that this structure may never be acquired by some individuals.

5.10 to 8.5. Individual rate of development plays a role within this period, but beyond it, we find uniform success. We stress the length of this 'potential learning' period for these two constructions because, as will be seen below, for pronominalization we will find a very different situation. The dominant features, then, of the acquisition of *promise* and *easy to see* are uniform success in children from age 9 on (slightly earlier for *easy to see*), and a potential learning period of three to four years prior to this age during which acquisition is subject to individual variation.

For pronominalization, we find the simplest pattern of all (Table 5.1). With very few exceptions, children above 5.6 in our sample know the construction, and children below 5.6 do not. This is quite a different situation from our other constructions. The most obvious distinction, namely that this construction is learned so much earlier than the others, is only part of its difference, and not the most interesting part. What distinguishes this acquisition from the others most significantly is the rapidity and uniformity with which it apparently takes place. Almost all our children start getting this construction right at about the same age. It seems to 'come in' at about 5.6, without being subject to the fairly extensive individual variations in rate of development which affect the acquisition of our other constructions. We suggested in §4 (D) that this difference may be related to the more basic nature of the principles of pronominalization in the language in general, as contrasted with the greater specificity of our other constructions which depend on particular lexical items. The basic principles of the language may be acquired more uniformly across children, perhaps at a certain level of maturation, whereas the more specialized constructions vary more with the individual. The dominant feature of the acquisition of pronominalization, then, is success after 5.6, failure before 5.6, and strong uniformity among the children in keeping to this pattern.

In summary, our four constructions may be characterized as follows:

1. *Promise* and *easy to see:* mixed period from age 5.6 to 9, success from age 9 on
2. *Ask:* mixed at all ages
3. *Pronominalization:* failure before age 5.6, success from 5.6 on

We can now turn to an analysis of the coordinated data and consider the children's successes and failures with the various constructions in terms of individual rate of development. This analysis includes our results for *ask/tell, promise* and *easy to see,* for which age of acquisition varies considerably, and omits pronominalization, which is not relevant to general developmental rate in that age of acquisition appears to be uniform.[11] In our sample at least, pronominalization apparently is not subject to individual developmental rate as are the other three constructions.

Our results show a high correlation of successes for the three constructions. Clearly a child who succeeds with one construction tends to succeed with the others as well. Figures 5.1 and 5.2 show this correlation in the children's performance. The children are organized according to the *ask/tell* stage into which they fall,[12] and the percentage of children in each stage who succeed at *promise* and *easy to see* is shown. Figure 5.1 shows the percentage of children who succeed at *each* of the other constructions, and Figure 5.2 shows the percentage of children who succeed at *both* of the other constructions. These figures show quite clearly the increased successes of children at higher *ask/tell* stages, irrespective of the age of the child. Children of all ages appear at each *ask/tell* stage:

Stage A–B:     5.0–7.6
Stage C:       5.2–10.0
Stage D:       6.9–8.8
Stage E:       5.10–9.9

and yet we find a significant increase in success with the other two constructions as we move up through the *ask/tell* stages. None of the children in stage A–B has both of the other constructions right, whereas almost all of the stage E children do. This correlation indicates that linguistic development apparently proceeds at a comparable pace for a variety of structures, and that in terms of acquisition, rate of development is, within limits, a stronger factor than age.

One final point concerning order of acquisition. We noted in §4 (C) that there is a relation between two of our structures, *promise* and *ask*, concerning subject assignment to infinitival complement verbs following these two verbs. Both *promise* and *ask* require the same linguistic process for complement subject assignment, namely

11. The three exceptions in our sample to the regular pronominalization pattern (see Table 5.1, ages 5.2', 6.10, 8.10) do show a relationship to general development. 5.2', who succeeds at pronominalization, succeeds equally with the other constructions, and 6.10 and 8.10, who fail at pronominalization, fail elsewhere as well.

12. Stages A and B are combined because of their similarity, and because of the tentative status of stage B.

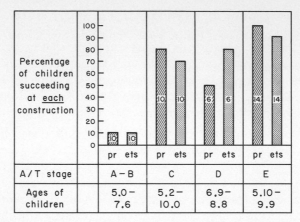

**Figure 5.1.** Percentage of Children at Each *ask/tell* Stage Who Succeed at *Promise* and *Easy to See* Tests. The number of children in each stage is indicated by the number inside each bar. The age range of the children in each stage is given across the bottom of the figure.

that the subject from the main clause, rather than the object, be selected as subject of the complement verb. In §4(C) we discussed the greater complexity of *ask* as compared to *promise* with respect to this process, and hypothesized that the *ask* construction would be learned later than the *promise* construction. Here we find that in fact this is the case. Every child as stage E (which indicates success with

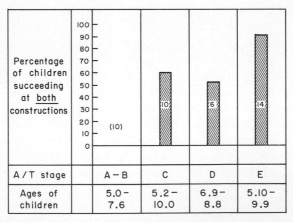

**Figure 5.2.** Percentage of Children at Each *ask/tell* Stage Who Succeed at Both *Promise* and *Easy to See* Tests. The number of children in each stage is indicated by the number inside each bar. The age range of the children in each stage is given across the bottom of the figure.

the complex *ask* construction) succeeds also with *promise* (see the 100% column in Figure 5.1, rightmost box). A child may know *promise* without knowing *ask*, as indicated in Figure 5.1 by the success columns for children in stages A through D, but he does not know *ask* without knowing *promise*. Our results confirm that he learns to apply this linguistic process in the simpler case first, and only then proceeds to use it in the more complex case.

# 6 Summary

We have studied children's acquisition of four syntactic structures that are considered candidates for late acquisition according to criteria of syntactic complexity:

| Structure | Difficulty |
|---|---|
| 1. John is easy to see. | 1. subject of sentence<br>subject of *see* |
| 2. John promised Bill to go. | 2. subject of *go* |
| 3. John asked Bill what to do. | 3. subject of *do* |
| 4. He knew that John was going<br>to win the race. | 4. reference of *he* |

We tested the comprehension of these structures by forty children between the ages of 5 and 10. Considerable variation was found in the ages of children who knew the structures and those who did not, and we were able to draw the following conclusions about acquisition for the children in our sample. Structures 1, 2, and 3 are strongly subject to individual rate of development. Structures 1 and 2 are acquired between the ages of 5.6 and 9, and are known by all children 9 and over. Structure 3 is still imperfectly learned by some children even at age 10, and structure 4 is acquired fairly uniformly at about age 5.6.

The significance of these results lies in the surprisingly late acquisition of syntactic structures that they reveal, and in the differences that they bring to light concerning the nature of the linguistic

120

processes studied. Contrary to the commonly held view that a child has mastered the structures of his native language by the time he reaches the age of 6, we find that active syntactic acquisition is taking place up to the age of 9 and perhaps even beyond. Second, our observations regarding *order* and *rate* of acquisition for related structures in different children are in agreement with the findings of investigators who have worked with younger children. By tracing the child's orderly progress in the acquisition of a segment of his language, we are able to observe, for a set of related structures, considerable variation in rate of acquisition in different children together with a common, shared order of acquisition. Quite simply, although we cannot say just when a child will acquire the structures in question, we can offer a reliable judgment about the relative order in which he will acquire them. Third, we find several distinct patterns of acquisition in our study, each characteristic of one or more of the test constructions. These observed differences in the way the structures are acquired point up interesting distinctions in the nature of the structures themselves. Last, the methods and general approach of this study are shown to be fruitful for investigating questions of linguistic complexity. Children at the stage of language learning which borders on adult competence can offer valuable material for studying degrees of complexity that may be otherwise difficult to detect. The differences between their grammar and adult grammar can be described in terms of the adult linguistic system, and reflect the intricacies of that system. Our understanding of linguistic complexity in general can be enhanced by inquiring into the children's underlying competence and studying these differences.

# Bibliography

Austin, J. L. (1962). *How to Do Things with Words.* London: Oxford University Press.

Bloomfield, L. (1927). "Literate and Illiterate Speech." *American Speech, 2,* 432–439. Reprinted in D. Hymes (ed.), *Language in Culture and Society: A Reader in Linguistics and Anthropology.* New York: Harper and Row, 1964, pp. 391–396.

Chomsky, N. (1964). *Current Issues in Linguistic Theory.* The Hague: Mouton & Co.

Fodor, J. A., M. Garrett, and T. G. Bever (1968). "Some Syntactic Determinants of Sentential Complexity, II: Verb Structure." *Perception and Psychophysics, 3* (1968), 453–461.

Fraser, C., U. Bellugi, and R. Brown (1963). "Control of Grammar in Imitation, Comprehension and Production." *J. Verbal Learning and Verbal Behavior, 2,* 121–135.

Lees, R. B. (1960). "A Multiply Ambiguous Adjectival Construction in English." *Language, 36,* 207–221.

Luria, A. R., and F. I. Yudovich (1959). *Speech and the Development of Mental Processes in the Child.* London: Staples Press.

McNeill, D. (in press). "The Development of Language." In P. A. Mussen (ed.), *Carmichael's Manual of Child Psychology.* New York: Wiley.

Mehler, J., and Bever, T. (1967). "Cognitive Capacity of Very Young Children." *Science, 158,* no. 3797, pp. 141–142.

Rosenbaum, P. S. (1965). *A Principle Governing Deletion in English Sentential Complementation.* IBM Research Paper RC–1519, Yorktown Heights, New York.

Rosenbaum, P. S. (1967). *The Grammar of English Predicate Constructions.* Cambridge, Mass.: MIT Press.

Ross, J. R. (1967). "On the Cyclic Nature of English Pronominalization." In *To Honor Roman Jakobson,* The Hague: Mouton and Co., pp. 1669–1682.

Slobin, D. (1966). "Grammatical Transformations and Sentence Comprehension in Childhood and Adulthood." *J. Verbal Learning and Verbal Behavior, 5,* 219–227.

Slobin, D., (ed.) (1967). *A Field Manual for Cross-Cultural Study of the Acquisition of Communicative Competence.* Mimeographed. Berkeley: University of California.

Turner, E. and R. Rommetveit (1967). "Experimental Manipulation of the Production of Active and Passive Voice in Children." *Language and Speech,* 10 (3), 169–180.

Vendler, Z. (1968). *Adjectives and Nominalizations,* The Hague: Mouton & Co.

# INDEX